ALMA-TADEMA

ALMA-TADEMA

ACADEMY EDITIONS·LONDON

ACKNOWLEDGEMENTS

Thanks are due to the following galleries for permission to reproduce works in their collections: the City Art Gallery, Bristol (36); the Lady Lever Art Gallery, Port Sunlight (23); the City of Manchester Art Galleries (13, 42). We are particularly grateful to Sotheby's Belgravia for supplying and for allowing us to reproduce photographs in their possession.

To Josette

First published in Great Britain by
Academy Editions, 7 Holland Street, London W8

ISBN 85670 357 5

Printed and bound in Great Britain by
Acolortone Ltd., Ipswich

ALMA-TADEMA

'A marbellous painter,' quipped *Punch* on one occasion. This facetious remark contains more than an element of truth, for Alma-Tadema was a painter of marble *par excellence,* giving it a lustre and pearly translucency that deceives the eye even allowing for the small scale of most of his work. It was this remarkable skill in rendering materials — diaphanous draperies, animal skins, metal and delicate flowers that made Alma-Tadema famous and sought after.

His technical brilliance, allied to cosy domestic scenes of Roman and Pompeiian life, often betraying more than a hint of sentimentality and using thinly disguised Victorian models posed in languorous attitudes, assured his success. This was an art made for enjoyment and, not surprisingly, was avidly collected by Victorian businessmen. Yet, if Alma-Tadema's art contained no moral messages, it was at least painted with archaeological exactitude, to such an extent that he was awarded a R.I.B.A. Gold Medal in 1906 for his contribution to architecture.

This concern with realistic portrayal — including the tiniest details — and domestic genre scenes indicates a Northern heritage. Although his paintings are now associated with the high Victorian art of the late nineteenth century in England, Alma-Tadema was, in fact, Dutch. He was born Laurens Alma Tadema (Alma, a family name, was inserted at the request of his godfather) in Dronryp, a small village in the Dutch province of Friesland on 8th January 1836. In 1838 the family moved to Leeuwarden, the capital of the province, because Alma-Tadema's father had been appointed notary of the town. Two years later his father died, leaving his wife in impoverished circumstances.

Laurens had shown artistic ability from an early age; a story is told of his mother awaking him in the morning by pulling a string attached to his toe in order to allow him time for sketching before he went to school. Despite inclinations towards art, the young Alma-Tadema was destined for a career in law. Evidently he was not suited to legal studies, and it seems to have provoked some sort of crisis as he became seriously ill. In 1852, therefore, Alma-Tadema was allowed to enroll at the Antwerp Academy. His tutors here undoubtedly shaped his predilection for historical genre scenes. He first studied under Baron Gustave Wappers, leader of the Romantic faction in Antwerp and a painter of Flemish history scenes, then under De Keyser who further encouraged this type of painting, as did Joseph Laurens Dyckmans, Professor of Painting at the Academy. In addition Alma-Tadema spent hours of study in the library of the Professor of Archaeology, Louis de la Taye. Finally, in 1860, Alma-Tadema became a pupil of Baron Hendryk Leys, a famous history painter, at that time working on a series of frescoes in the Town Hall at Antwerp, illustrating events from the town's history. Leys believed in painting materials with convincing realism and once advised his student to paint a table leg, 'you could bark your shins on!' This lesson was obviously absorbed by Alma-Tadema.

Alma-Tadema's early works took as their subject matter obscure tales of Meroving- ian life, with titles such as *Clothilde at the Tomb of her Grandchildren* (1858) and *The Education of the Children of Clovis* (1860), both canvases already showing his unmis- takable attention to detail. In 1862 he briefly visited London where he spent much time studying the Elgin Marbles and Egyptian antiquities. The next phase of his career, perhaps understandably, covered Egyptian themes. *How the Egyptians amused themselves 3000 years ago* (1863) has a meticulously researched architectural setting of the time of Rameses II, culled presumably from the collection of the British Museum, as Alma- Tadema did not personally visit Egypt until 1902.

The turning point in Alma-Tadema's life comes in 1863 when he visited Italy on honeymoon with his first wife, the daughter of a French journalist. The ruins of Pom- peii and Herculaneum made a lasting impact on him. Here he could see at first hand, not only ancient architecture but also domestic utensils coming to light in the excavations in progress at the time. From 1865 onwards Alma-Tadema's art strove to recreate the daily life of Pompeii and Rome, using archaeologically exact settings (he made many sketches and collected documentary material in Pompeii) and adding a sparkling atmo- sphere which captures perfectly the warmth of the Mediterranean sun.

Alma-Tadema found a market for his pictures through Ernest 'Prince' Gambart , possibly the most influential of all Victorian art dealers. Gambart was apparently de- liberately misdirected to the painter's studio by a friend of Alma-Tadema's while he was on his way to visit Dyckman's studio. This ruse proved to be a great success, for Gambart admired Alma-Tadema's work and saw the commercial possibilities of his evocations of classical life. The combination of the two men — for Alma-Tadema himself was an astute businessman — assured his reputation on an international scale.

His work became popular in England and in 1870 he went to live there permanently taking with him his two small daughters, Laurence and Anna. His first wife had since died and the following year he remarried. His new bride was Laura Theresa Epps, the daughter of a wealthy doctor. Laura was a model in many of his pictures and was also a competent pupil, although her paintings were much closer to the style of seventeenth century Dutch art than those of her husband. Alma-Tadema further cemented his ties with his new country by changing his name to the anglicised version of Lawrence.

From the 1870s until his death in 1912, Alma-Tadema's work was dominated by the classical genre scenes for which he is most famous. Their silvery light effects were achieved by using a white ground and building up the dark tones, a method similar to that practised by the Pre-Raphaelites. Interestingly, the sunlit quality of these works, as in for example, *Silver Favourites* of 1903, was purely painterly and not aided by varnishes. Alma-Tadema once remarked, 'I never varnished a painting yet but once, and that turned out to be a failure.'

Alma-Tadema's colour complements these sunny idylls — the Pompeiian reds of the 1860s and 1870s superseded by pastel shades, white and grey marble set against sapphire blue seas with sudden splashes of crimson or rose pink as in *Expectations* of 1885. The curving marble bench in this picture frequently appeared in other works although usually seen from a different angle. Another favourite prop was his studio seat, designed with an Egyptian motif on one side and a Pompeiian on the other. This appears — displaying its Pompeiian side — in *Vain Courtship* of 1900.

Alma-Tadema obviously experimented with compositional effects for no two pictures, however similar, are exactly alike. Most daring, perhaps, is the dizzy perspective of *A Coign of Vantage* (1895), where the elegantly posed women await the return of their loved ones, whose boat is seen far below the marble balcony upon which they are perched. This type of effect — particularly the wide panoramas — is often quoted as influencing the early epic films.

Alma-Tadema himself made extensive use of the relatively new art of photography, which no doubt accounts for many of these unusual spatial illusions. He also used photographs as references and owned an enormous collection of 168 folios carefully arranged in sections; these included ancient architecture, classical ornamental design and jewellery.

Another example of this extraordinarily methodical approach to his work is shown by his habit of applying opus numbers to all his pictures (the last one is Op.CCCCVIII), thereby restricting forgeries and making it possible to reconstruct the exact chronological sequence of all his work.

Every detail of Alma-Tadema's paintings is depicted with painstaking care, equalling the miniaturist's art. He would even offer visitors a magnifying-glass with which to examine his work! Each flower is a replica of a real specimen, and he went to such lengths to achieve naturalism that when painting *The Roses of Heliogabalus* (1888) in the winter, he had roses brought from the French Riviera every week for four months to ensure that all the petals were accurately portrayed. Despite this concern for precision, his pictures are never pedantic and cannot be described as academic; indeed, they often display a coy sensuality as in *In the Tepidarium* (1881).

As he worked, so he lived. 'Tad,' as he was known to his friends, was an extrovert, a lover of parties and fond of jokes and puns — usually bad ones. The Alma-Tademas' 'At Homes' on Monday afternoons were famous. His houses were architectural extensions of his paintings. The most renowned was 17, later 42, Grove End Road, St. John's Wood, a 'veritable Pompeiian palace' whose doorway was an accurate copy of the entrance to the building of Eumachia in the forum at Pompeii, and bore the greeting 'Salve.' The colonnade around the garden pool, built by the French painter Tissot who originally owned the house, appears in many of Alma-Tadema's pictures.

Evidently Alma-Tadema regarded neither himself nor his art too seriously. He once appeared at the Institute of Painters in Watercolour Ball dressed as a Roman Emperor, crowned by a wreath of bluebells. His personality is an endearing one, for unlike many of his contemporaries, he was able to view his paintings objectively. The painter John Singer Sargent commented acidly, 'I suppose it's clever. Of course it *is* clever . . . but of course it's not art . . .' There were others who were less critical, and even more who were great admirers. Alma-Tadema was one of the richest and most successful of all Victorian and Edwardian artists, knighted in 1899 and awarded the Order of Merit in 1905. He died in Wiesbaden, Germany, where he had gone to recuperate from ill-health, on 25th June 1912 at the age of seventy-six, and was buried in the crypt of St. Paul's Cathedral alongside Landseer, Turner, Leighton, Millais, Poynter and Holman Hunt.

Alma-Tadema's pictures, painted for the pleasure and entertainment of his patrons, emanate *joie-de-vivre*. He probably never considered his art to be anything other than what it is — an art of escapism, idylls of luxury and indolence, reflecting the sort of life to which many would like to aspire, but few attain.

1

An Egyptian in his doorway
c. 1865 version of Op. XXVI
11x16½ in

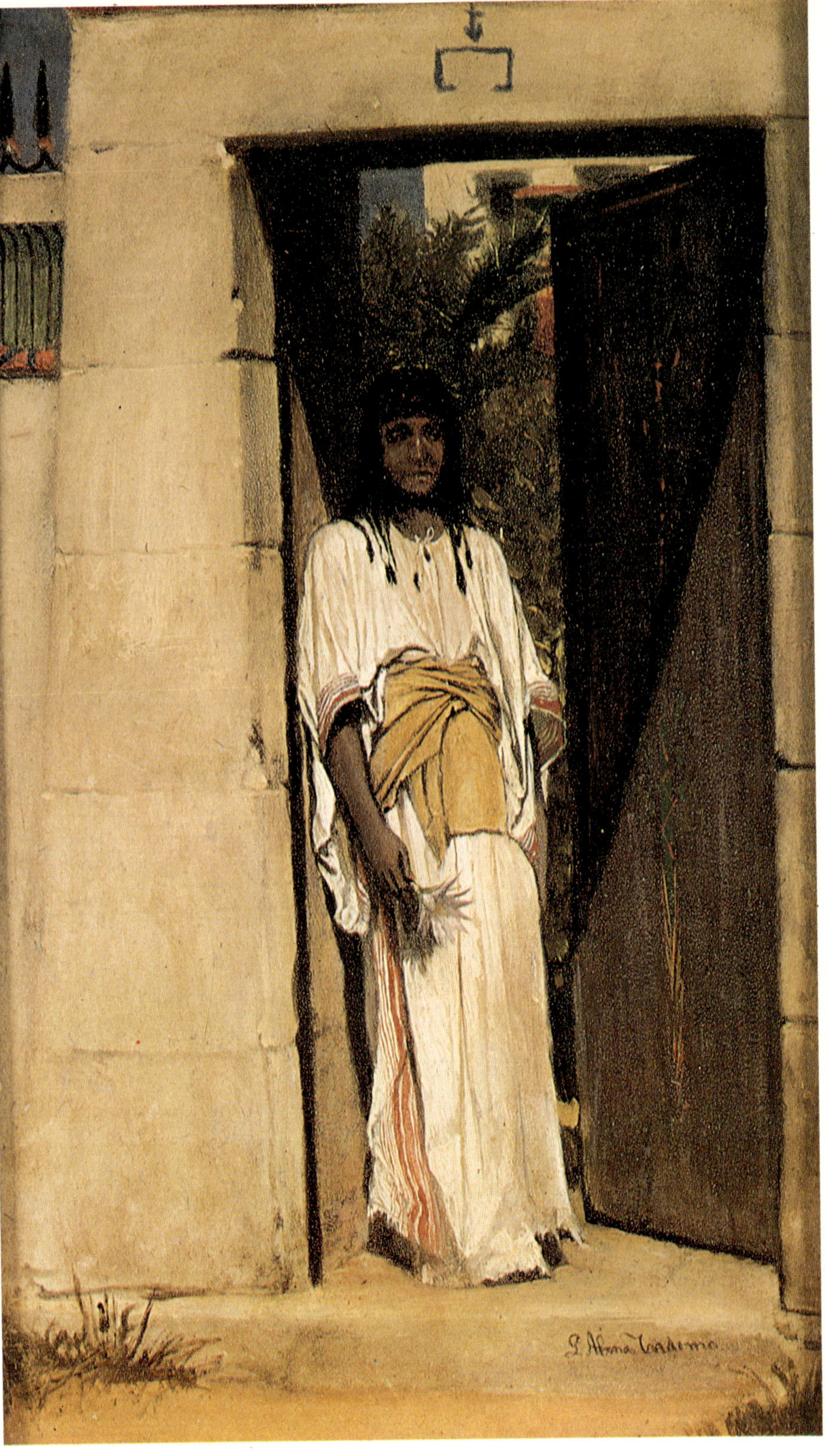

2

An Egyptian in his doorway
1865 Op. XXVI
11x16½ in

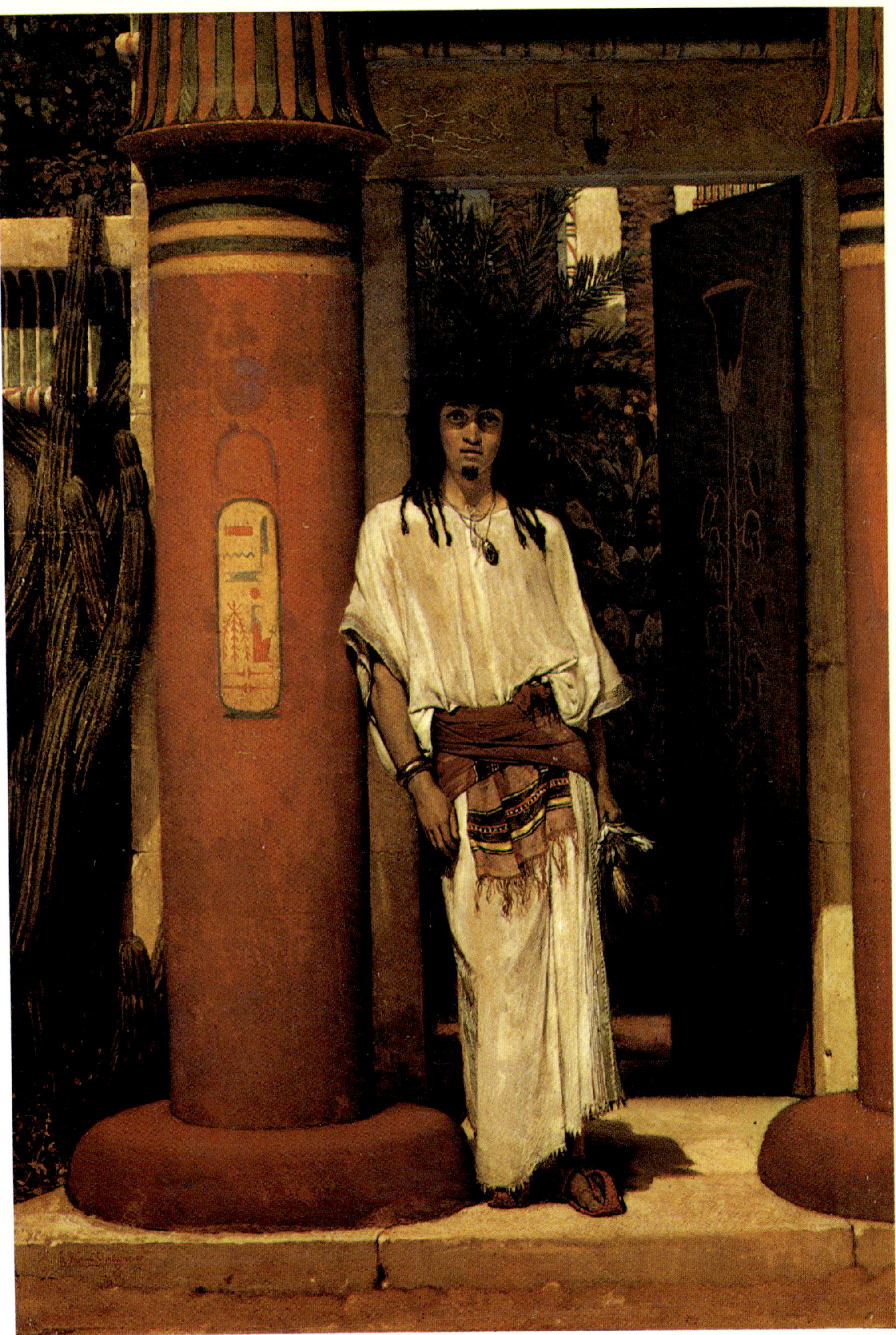

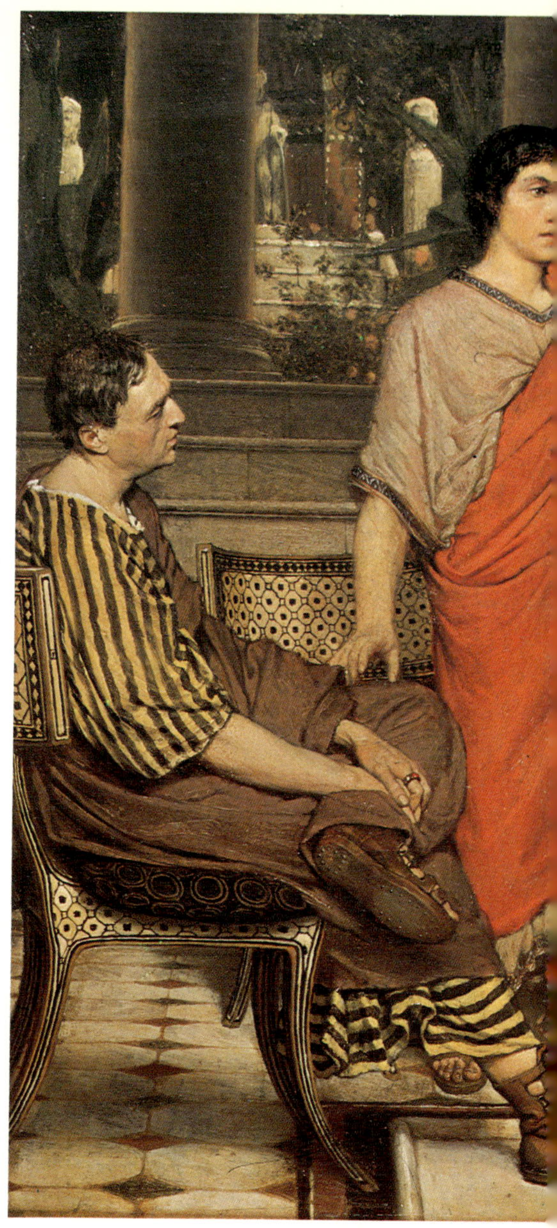

3

Catullus at Lesbia's
1865 Op. XXVII
15½x21½ in

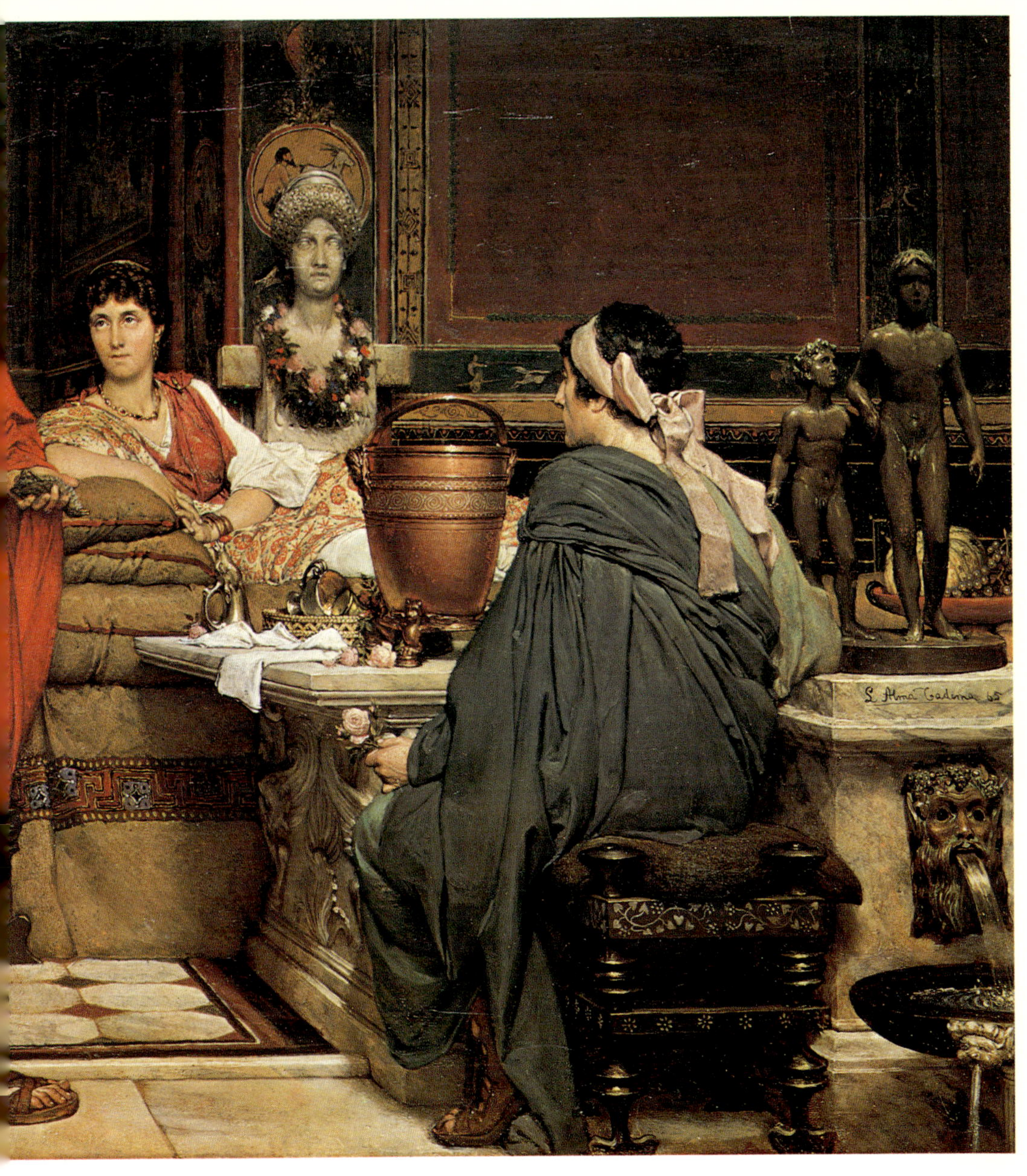

4

Agrippina with the Ashes of Germanicus
1866 Op. XXXVII
10¾x14¾ in

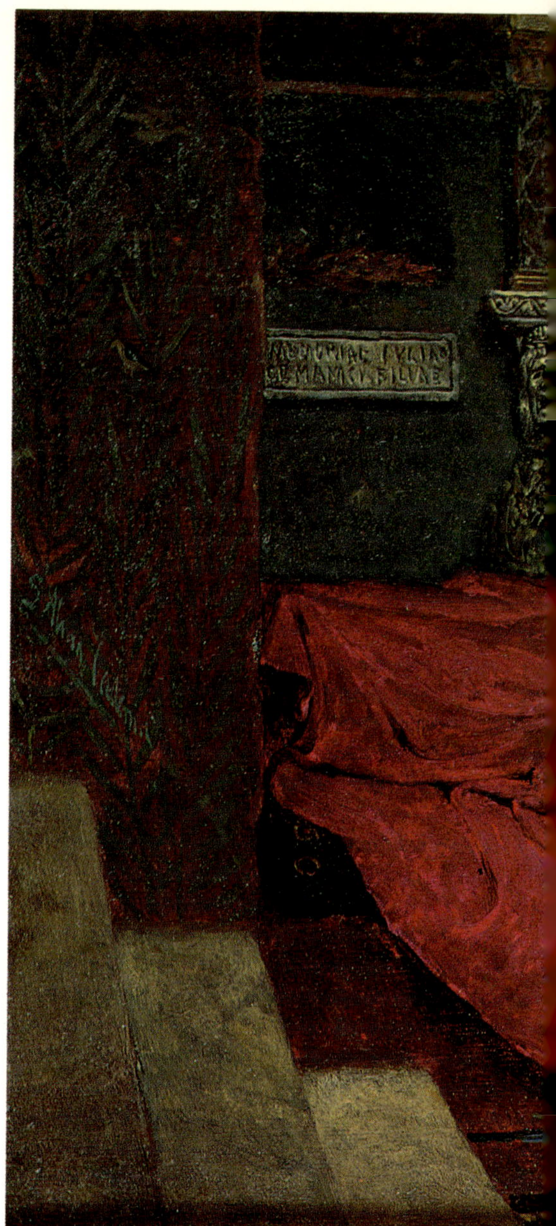

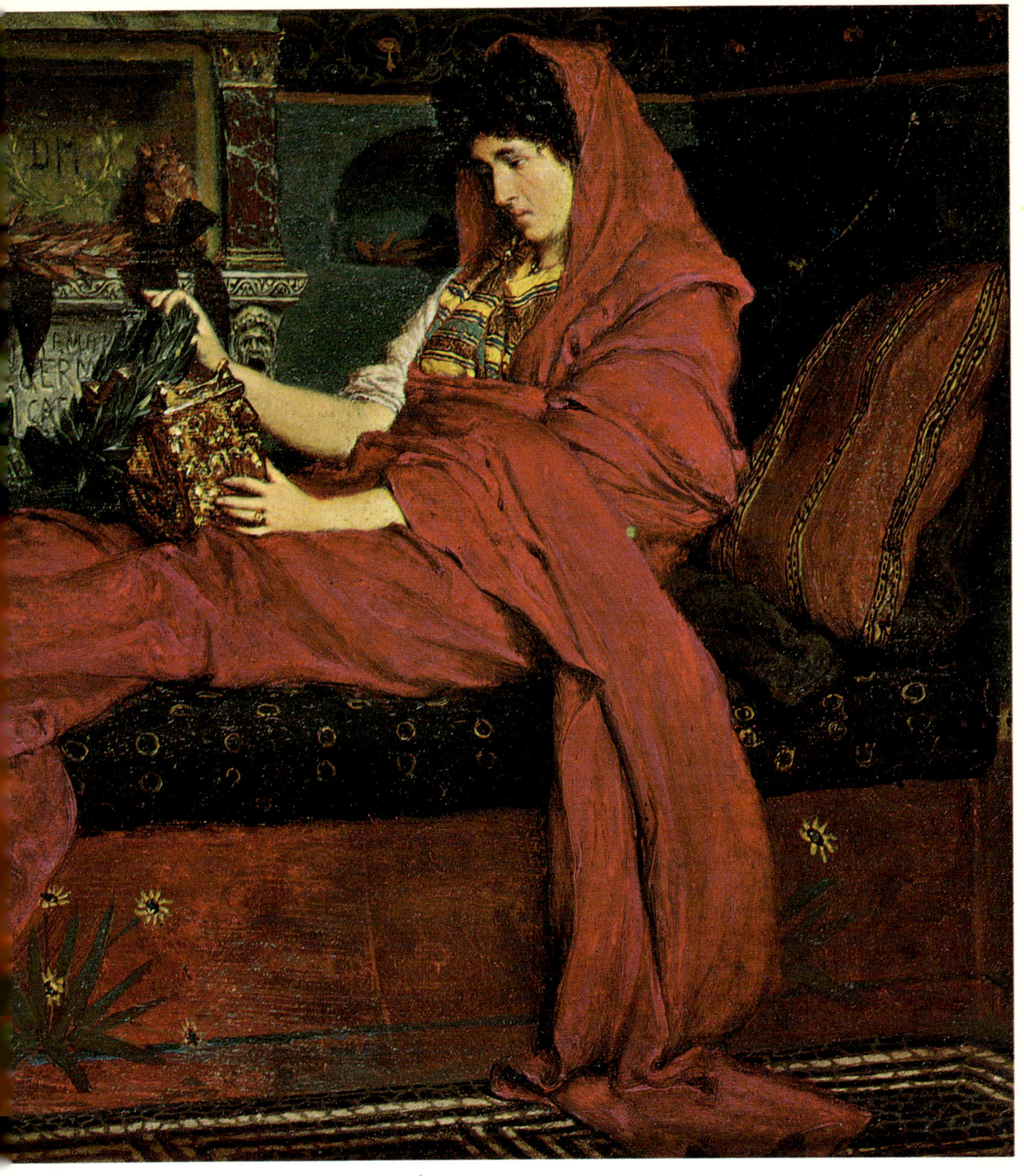

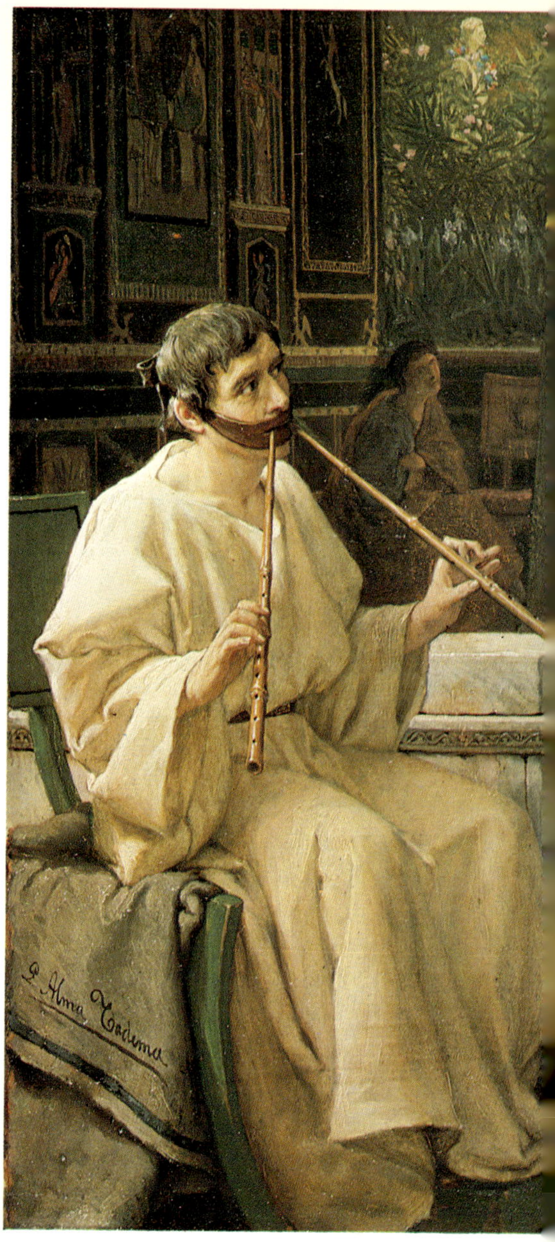

5

The Roman Dance
1866 Op. XXXIX
16¼x22¾ in

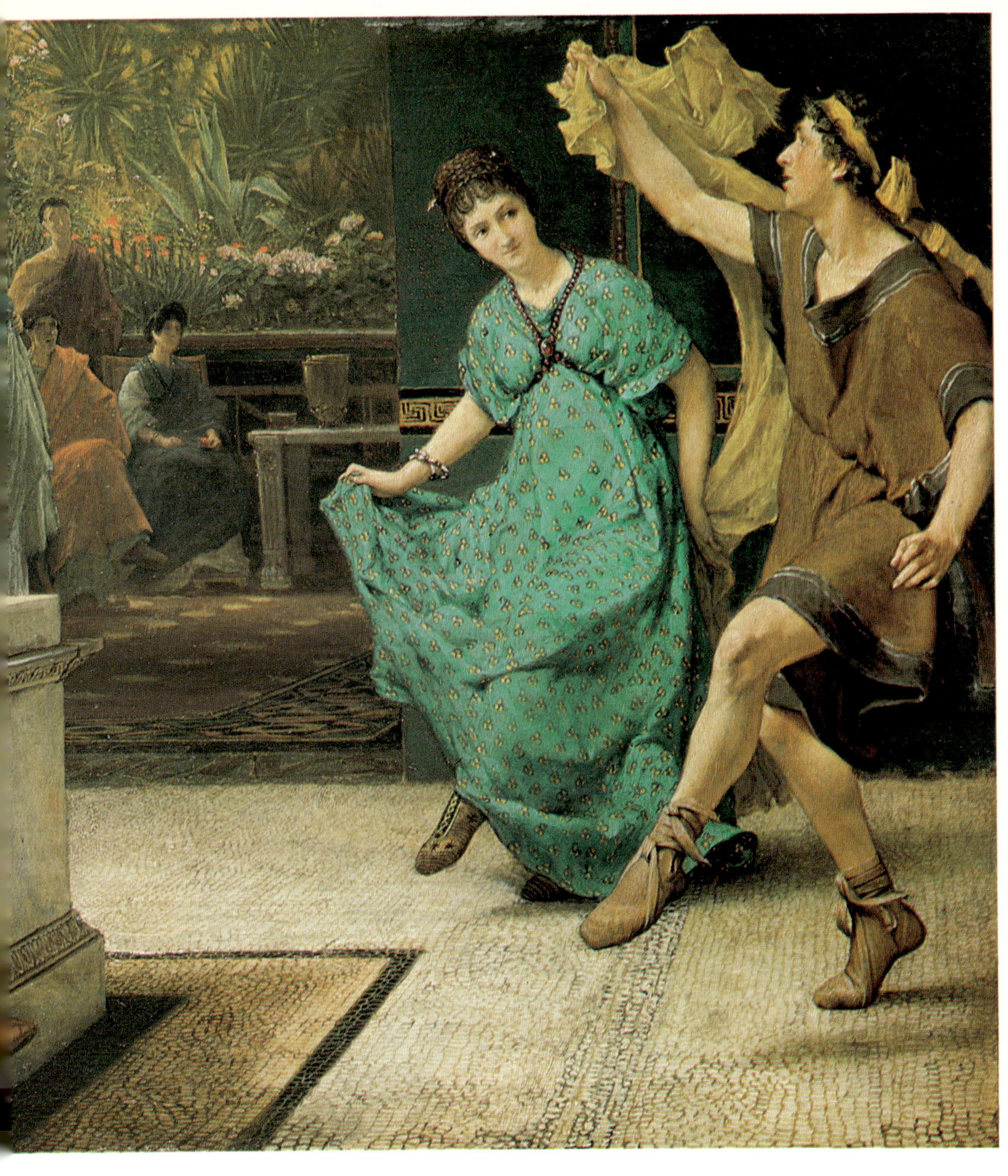

6

Lesbia
1866 Op. XL
25x19 in

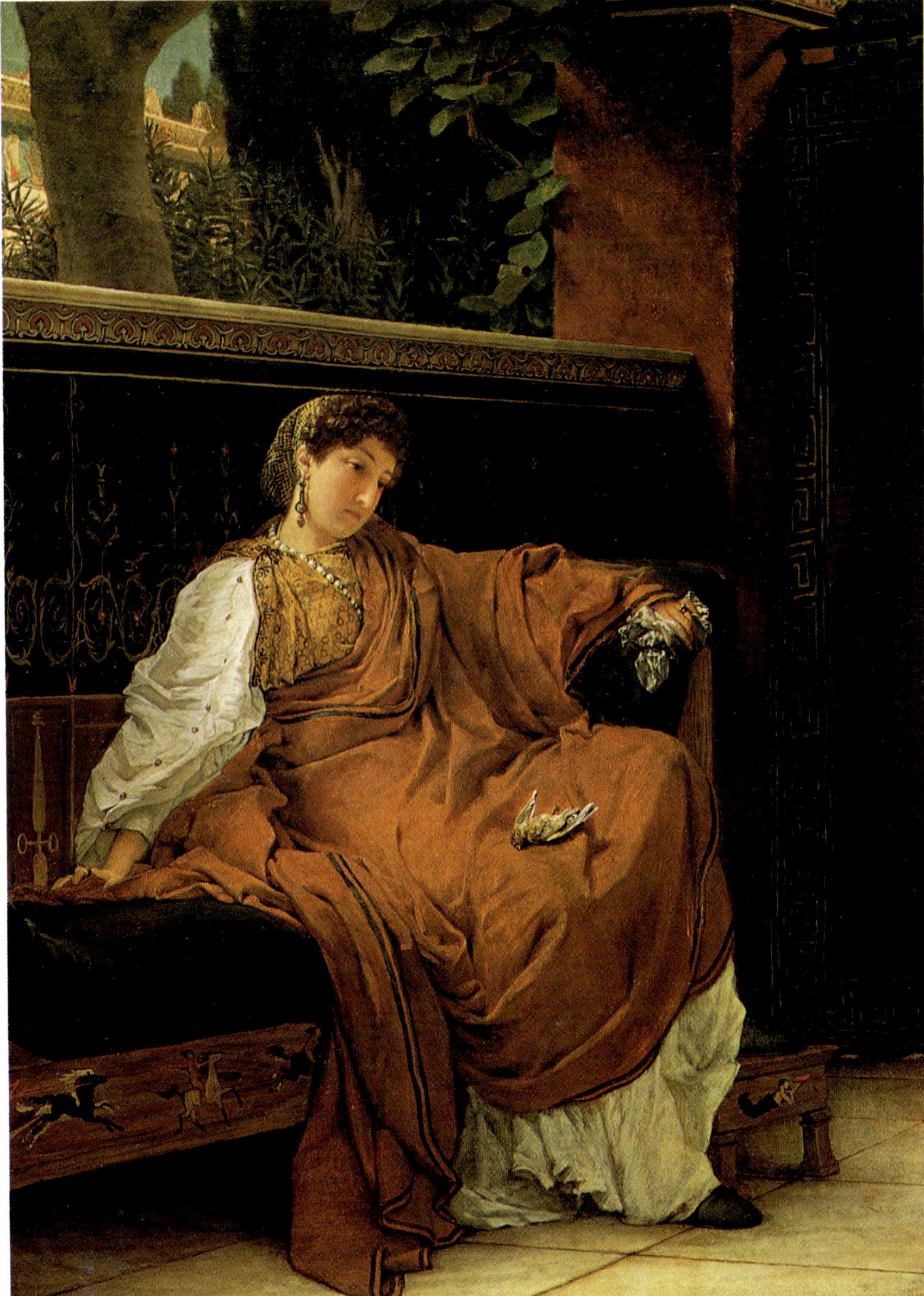

7

The Armourer's Shop
1866 Op. XLI
16¾x23¼ in

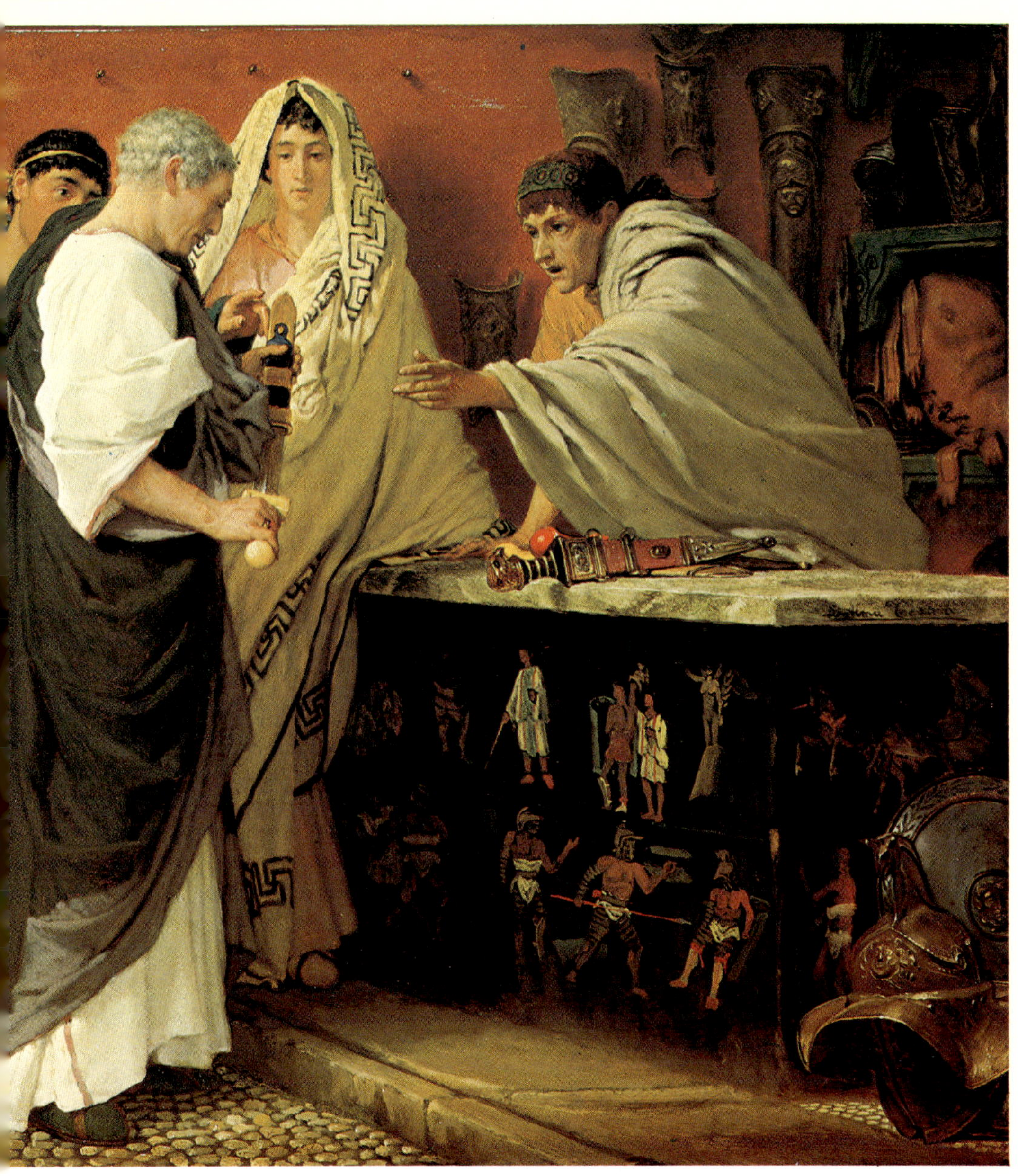

8

A Young Woman in a Garden
1866 Op. LIX
23x16¼ in

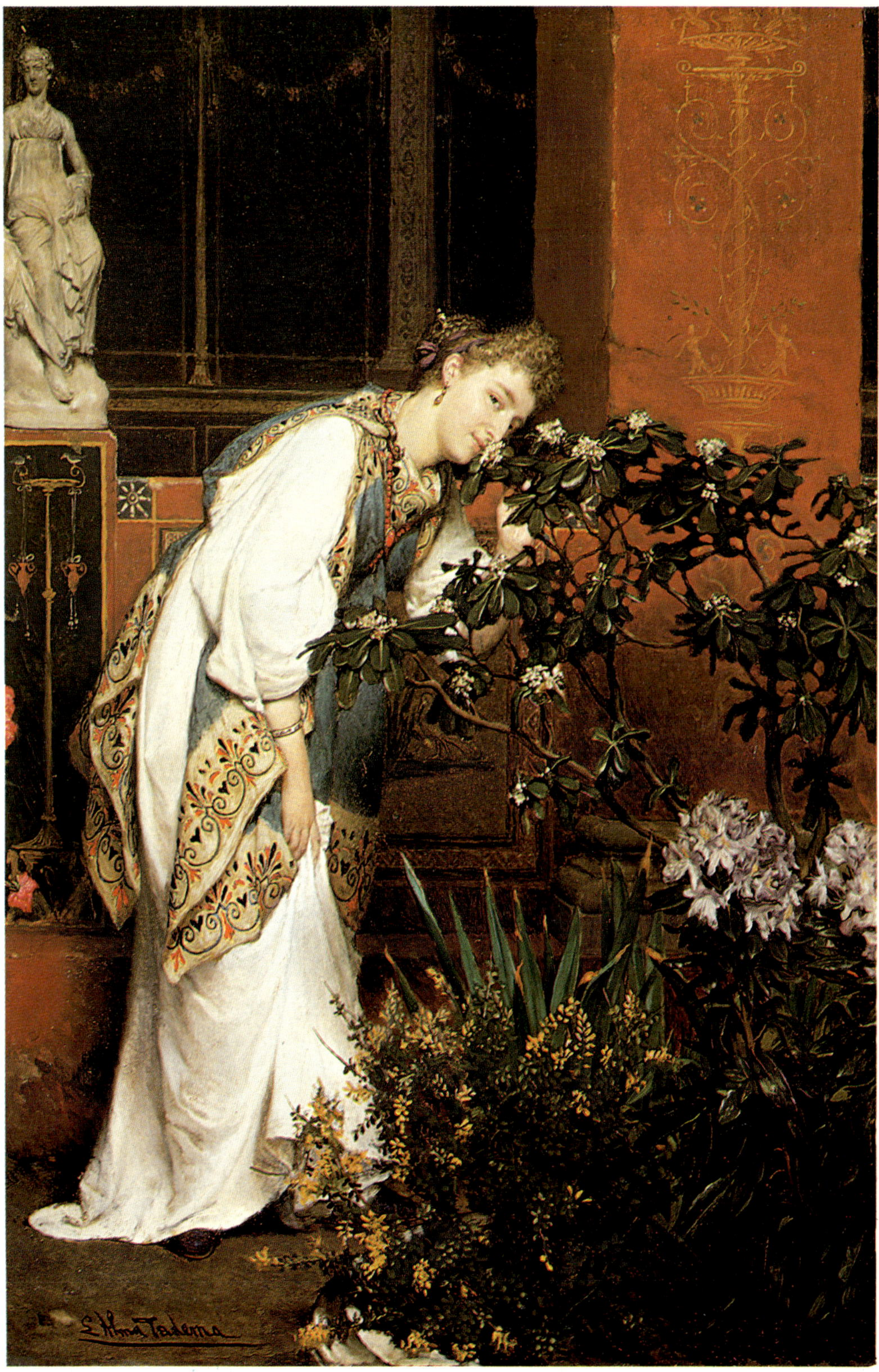

9

Glaucus and Nydia
1867 Op. XLVI
15½x25¼ in

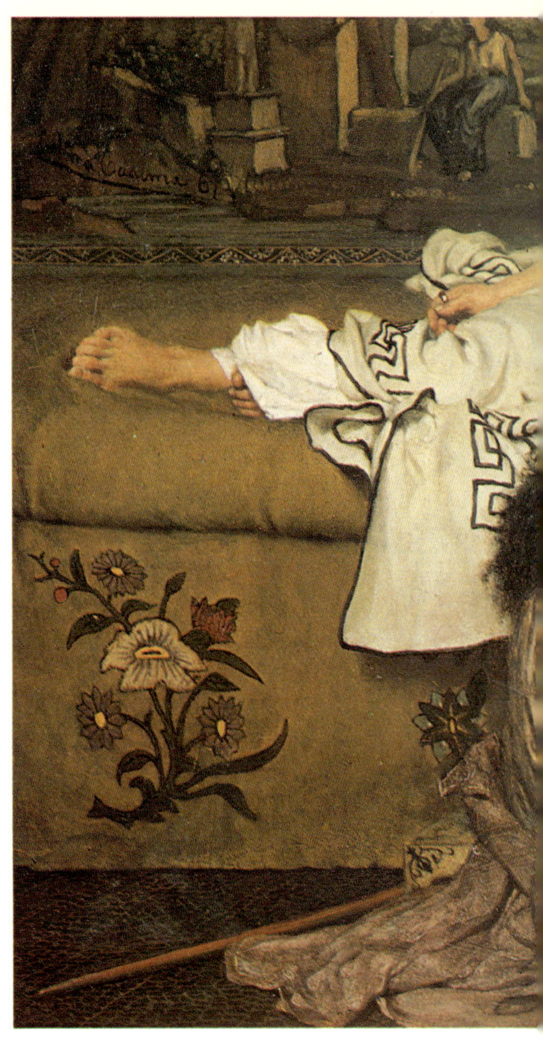

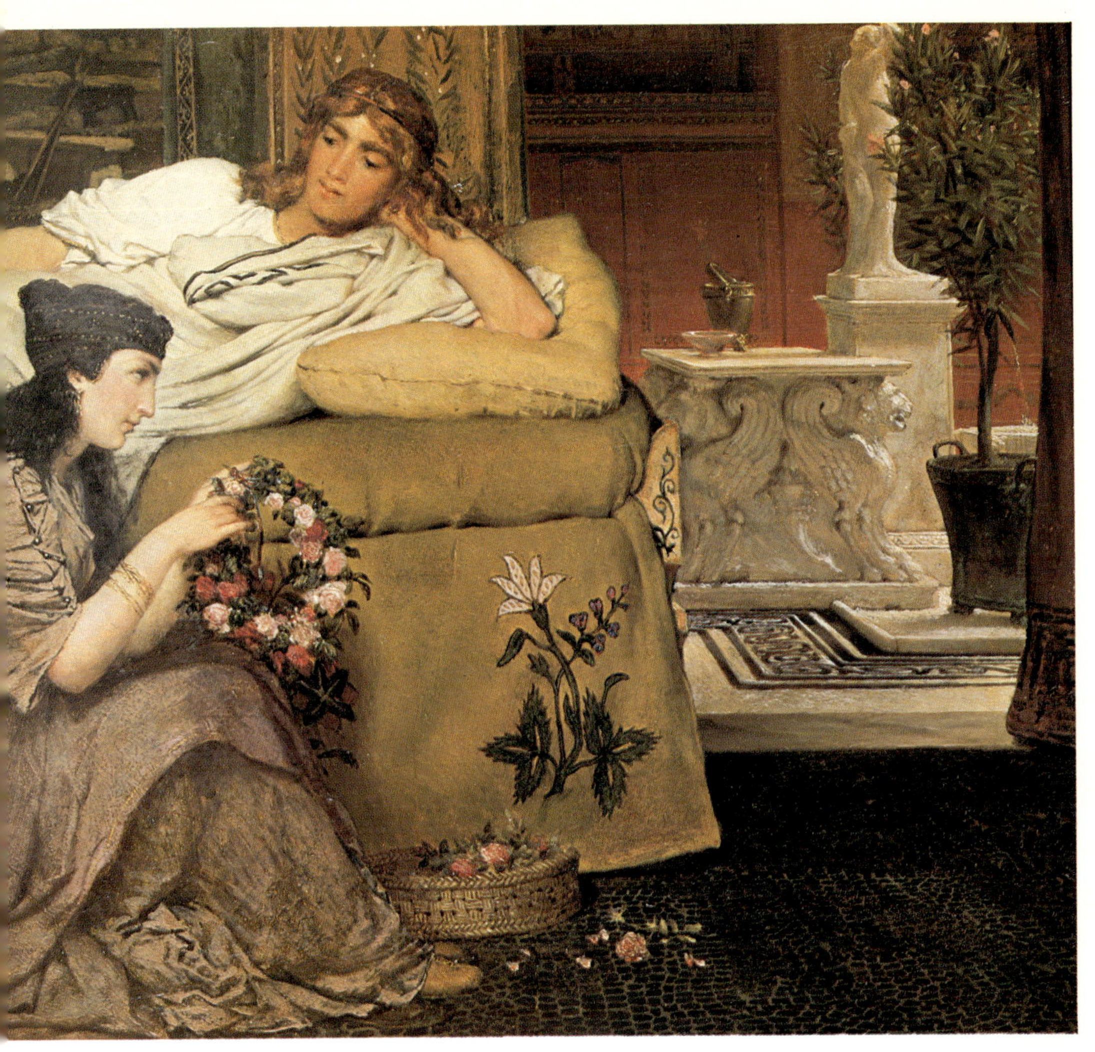

10

A Collector of Pictures
1867 Op. CLXI version of Op. CXVII
28x18¼ in

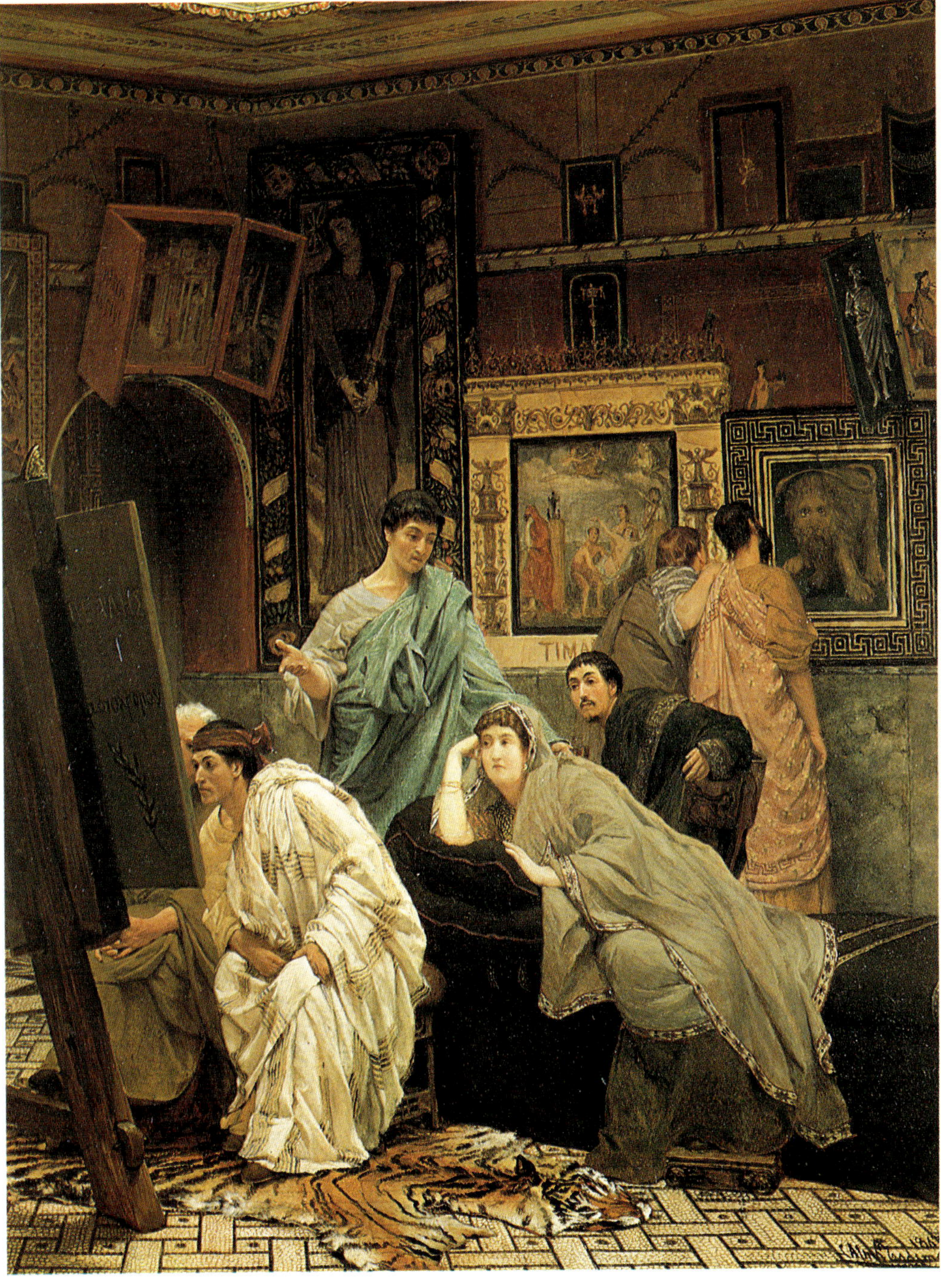

11

Taraninius Superbus
1867 Op. LI
22½x15 in

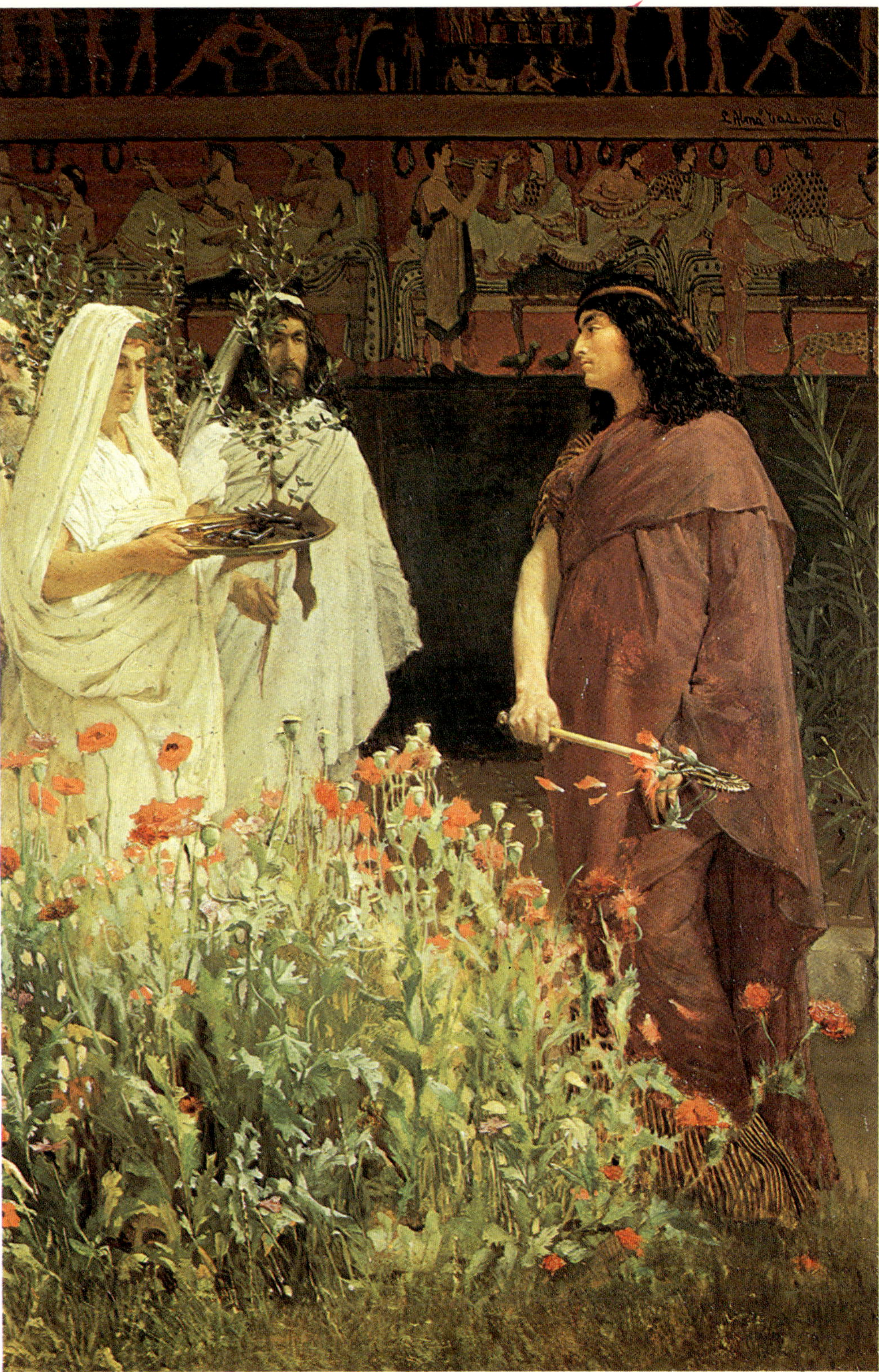

12

A Roman Family
1867 Op. LII
19x14 in

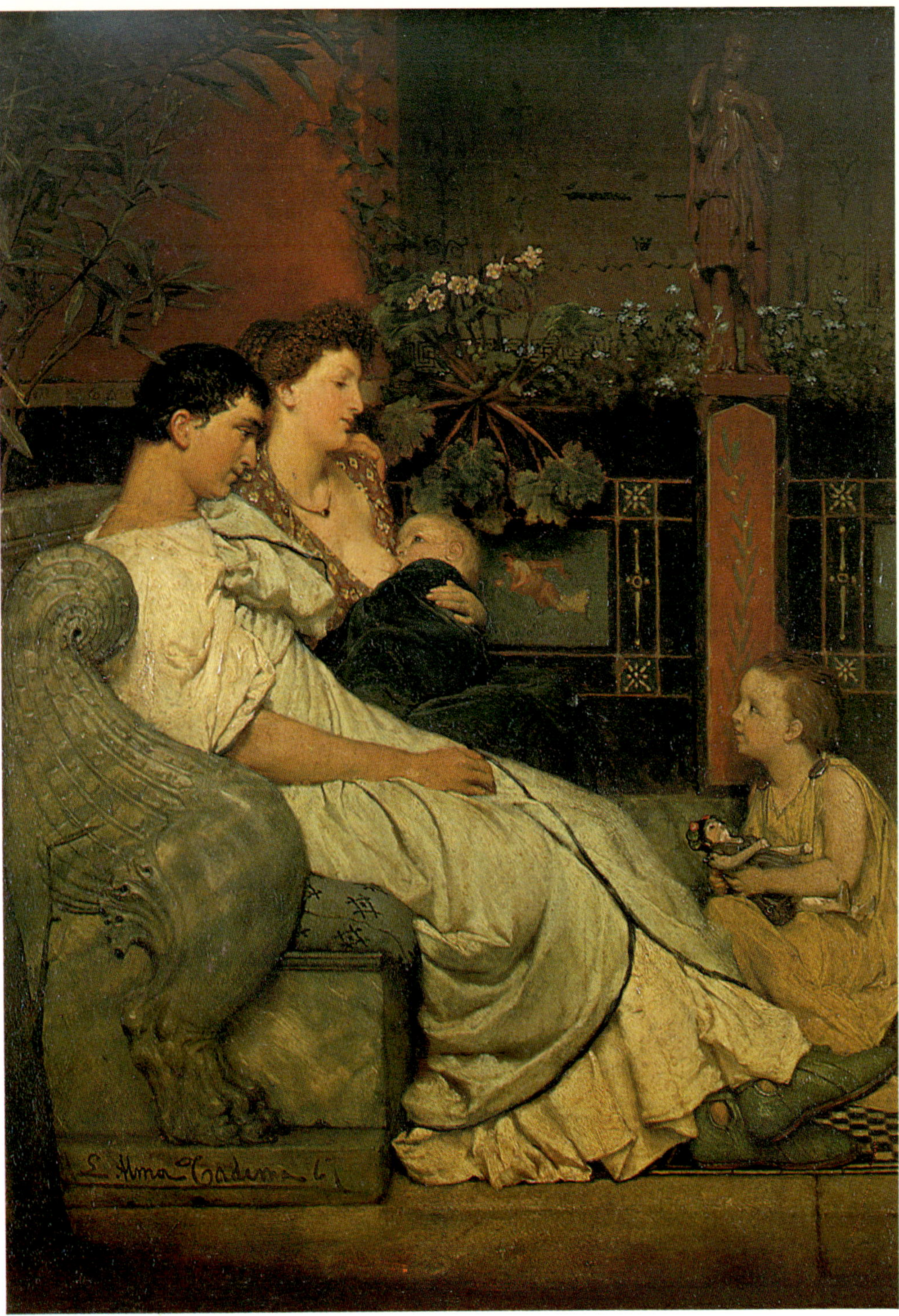

13

A Roman Flower Market
1868 Op. LXII (retouched 1911)
16½x22½ in

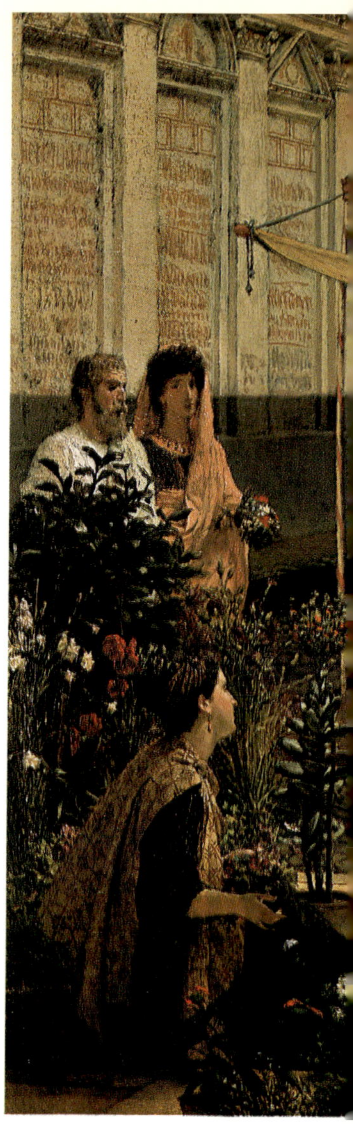

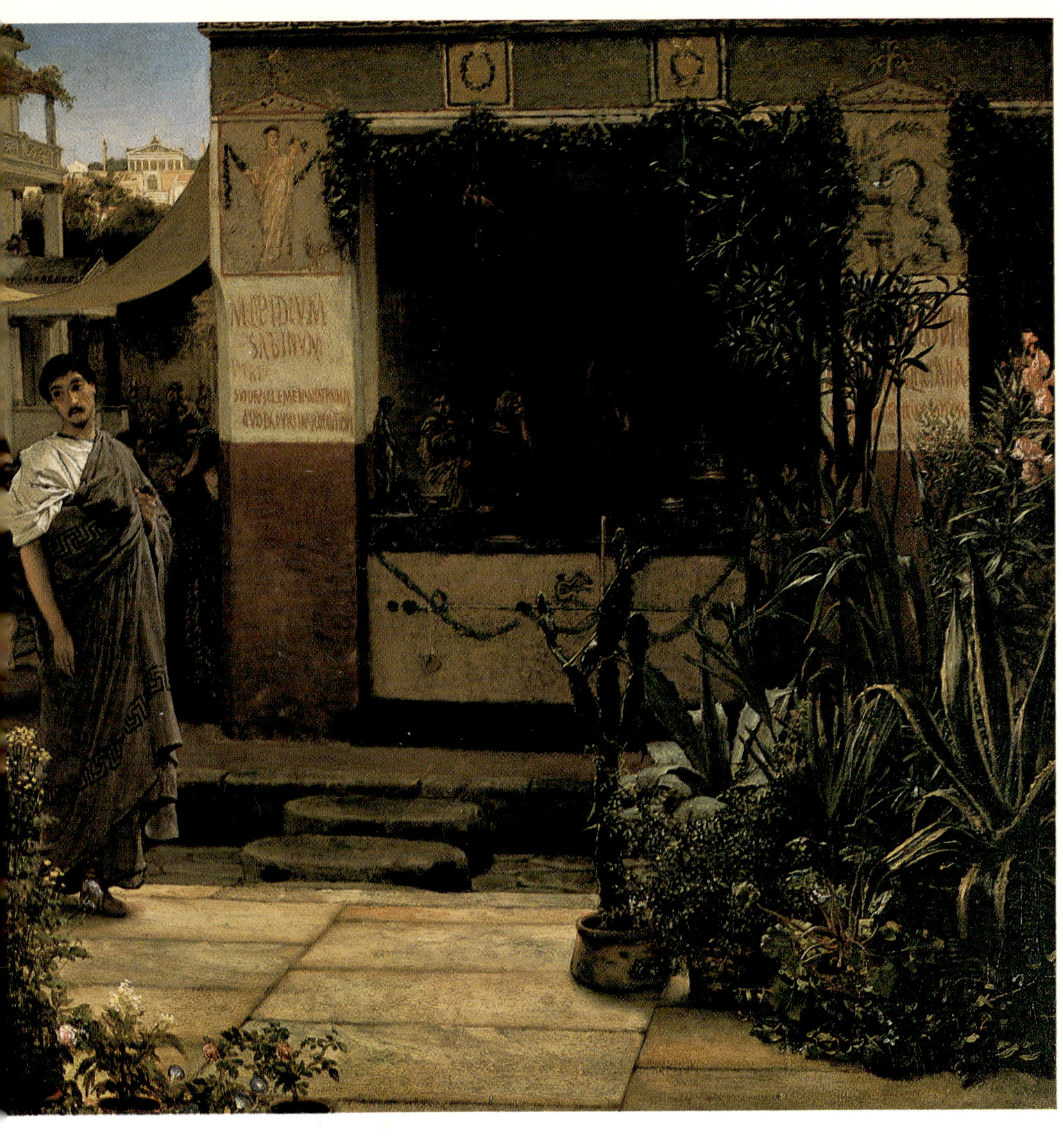

14

At Lesbia's
1870 Op. LXXX
15½x19 in

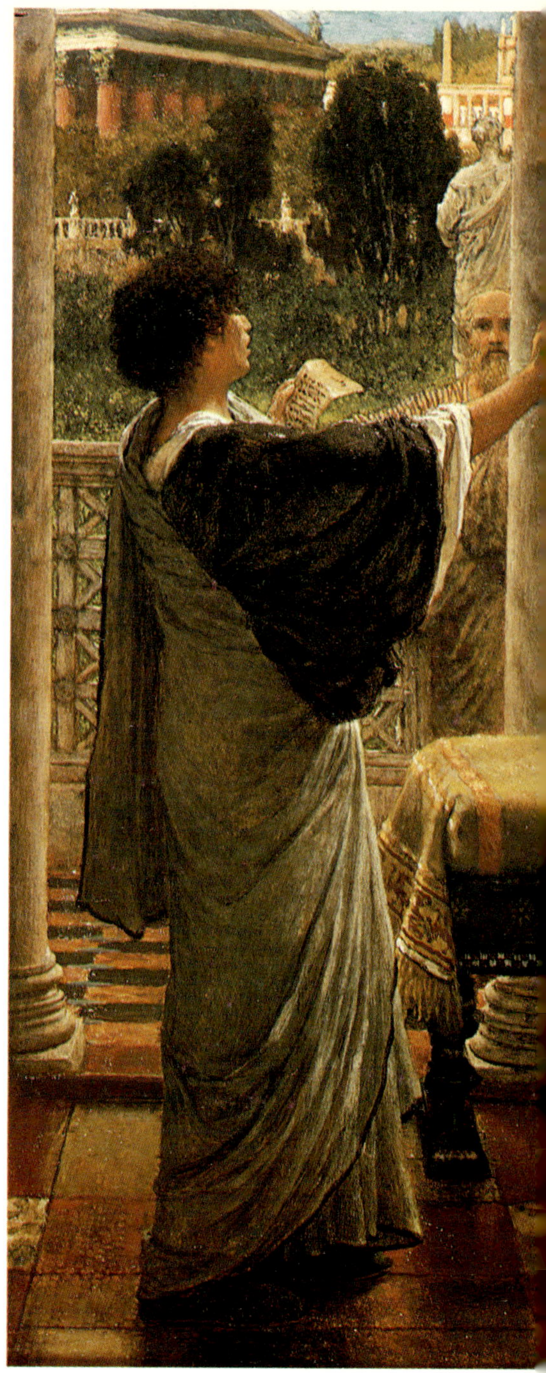

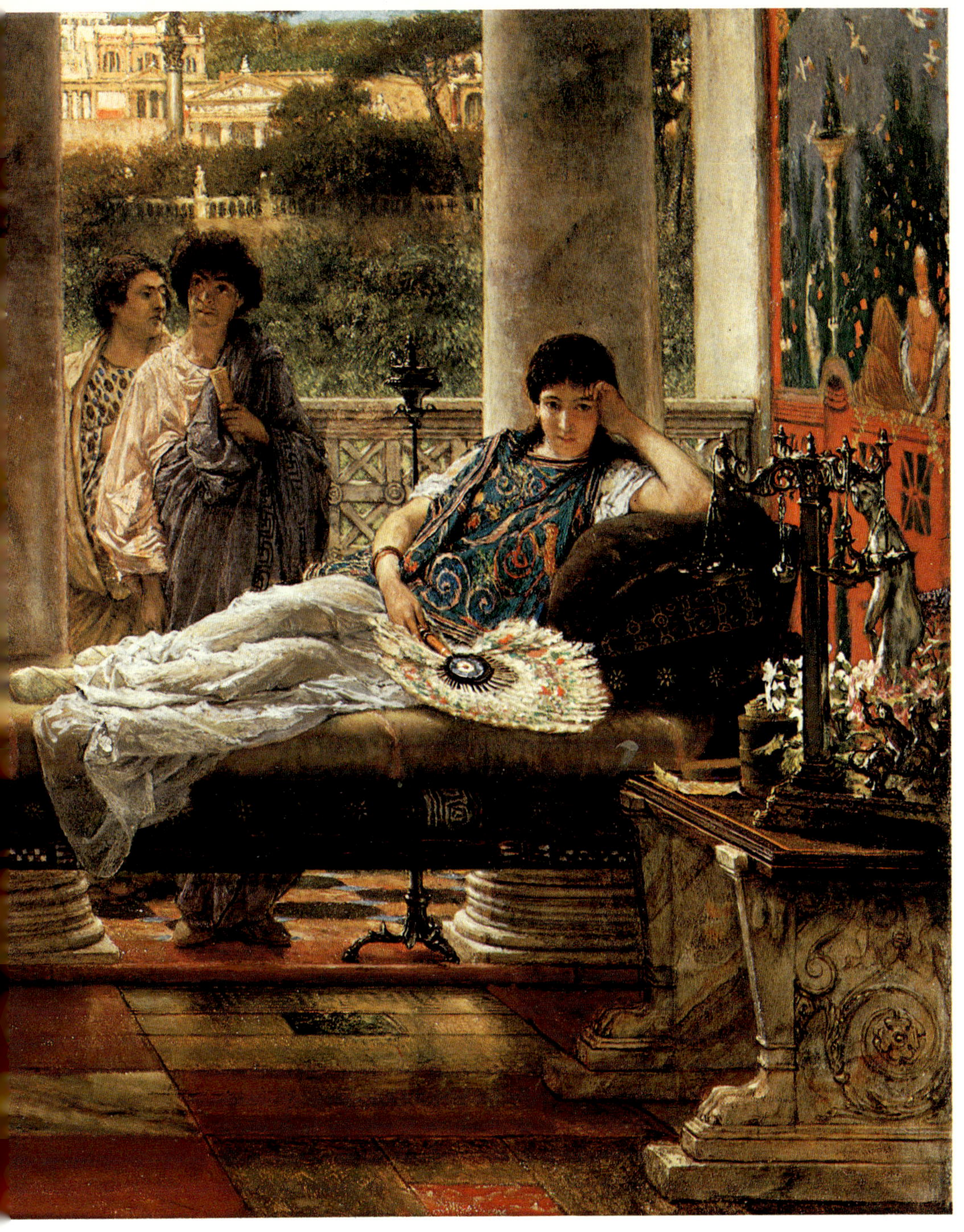

15

In the Temple
1871 Op. LXXXIX
35½x20½ in

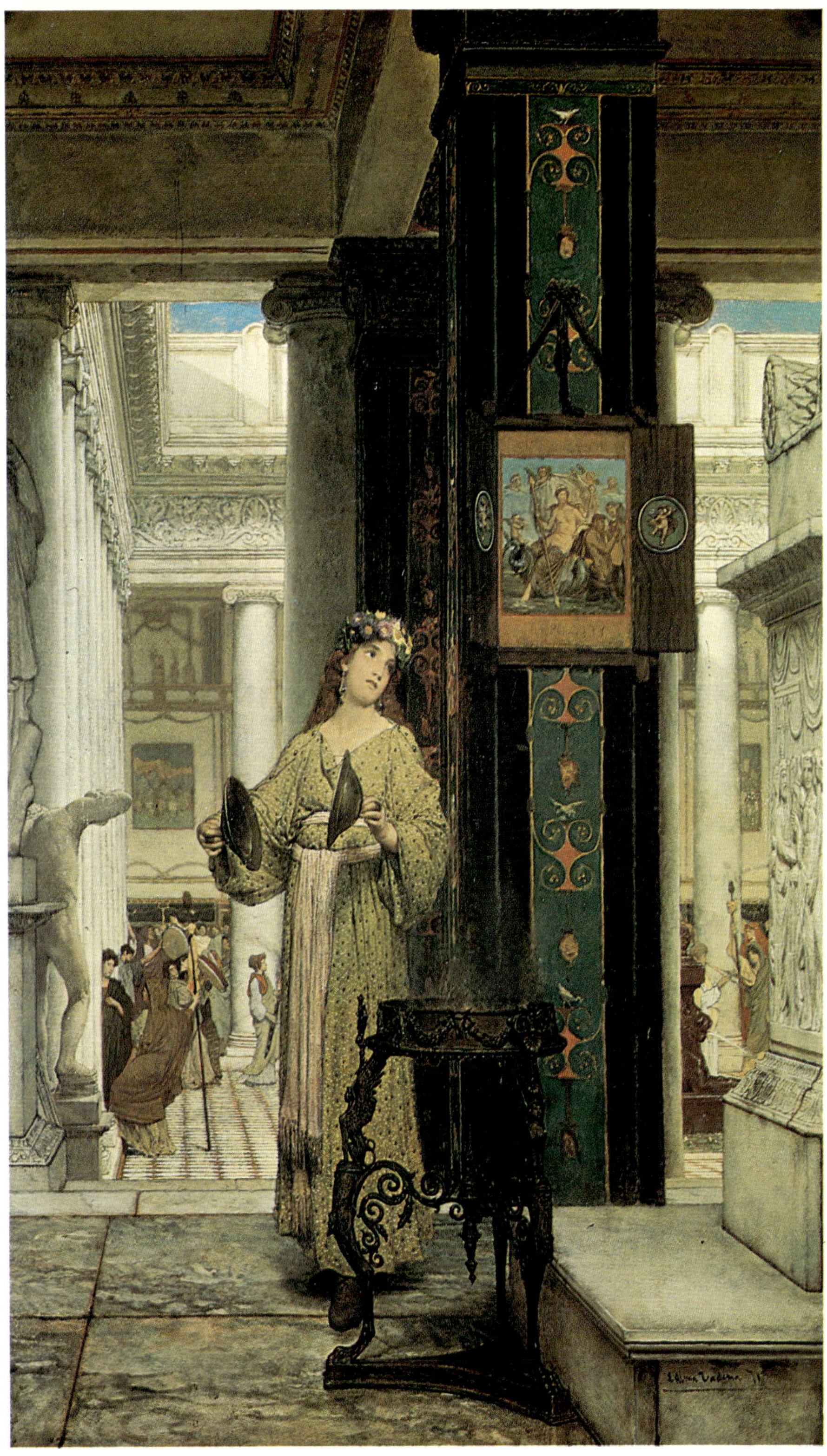

16

The Nurse
1872 Op. CV
17¼x23½ in

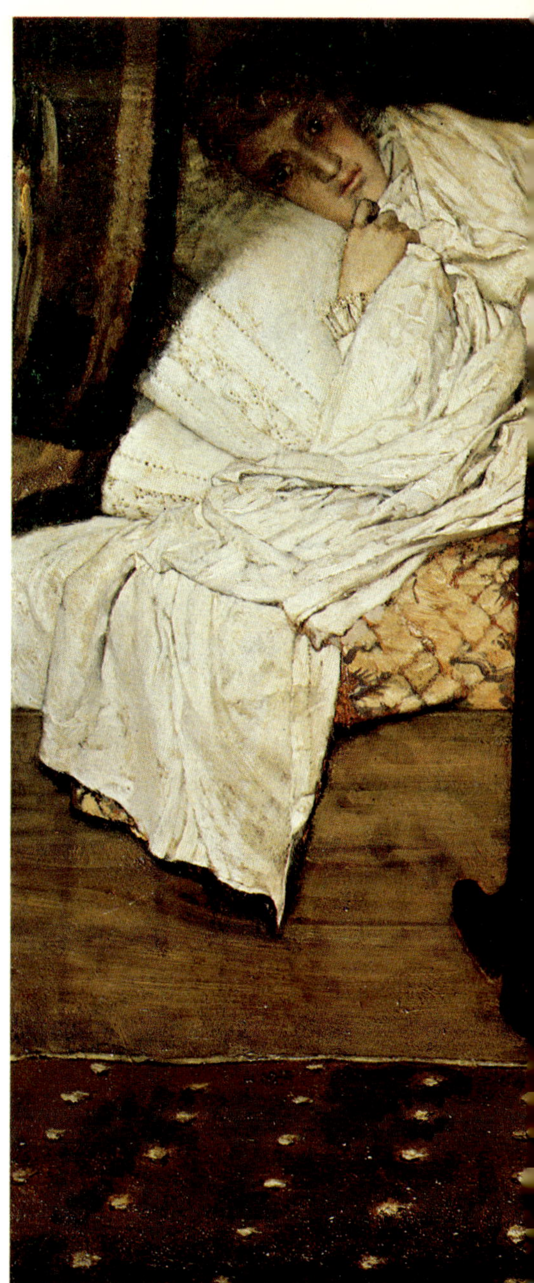

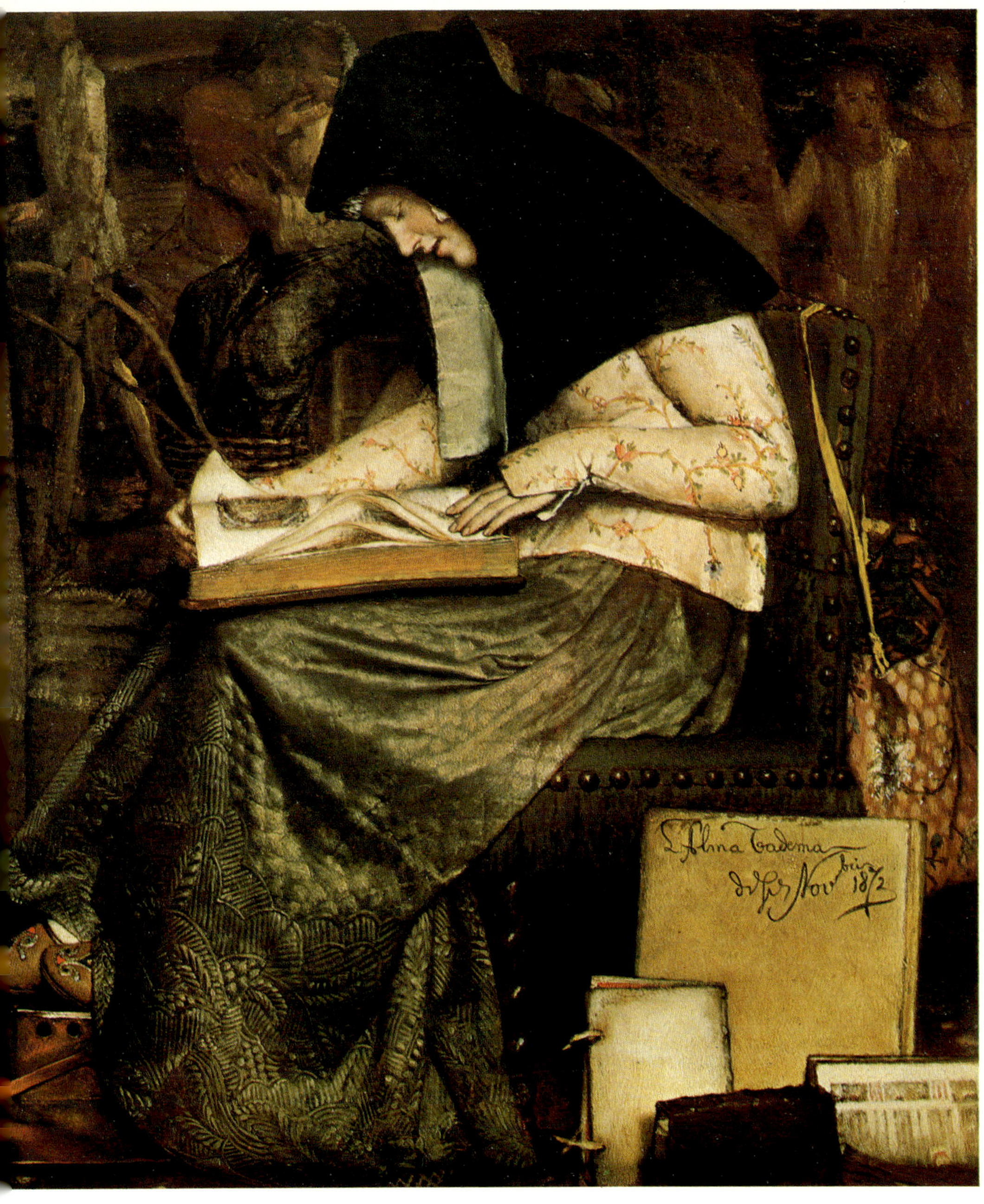

17

A Visit to the Studio
1873 Op. CXIII
26½x15¾ in

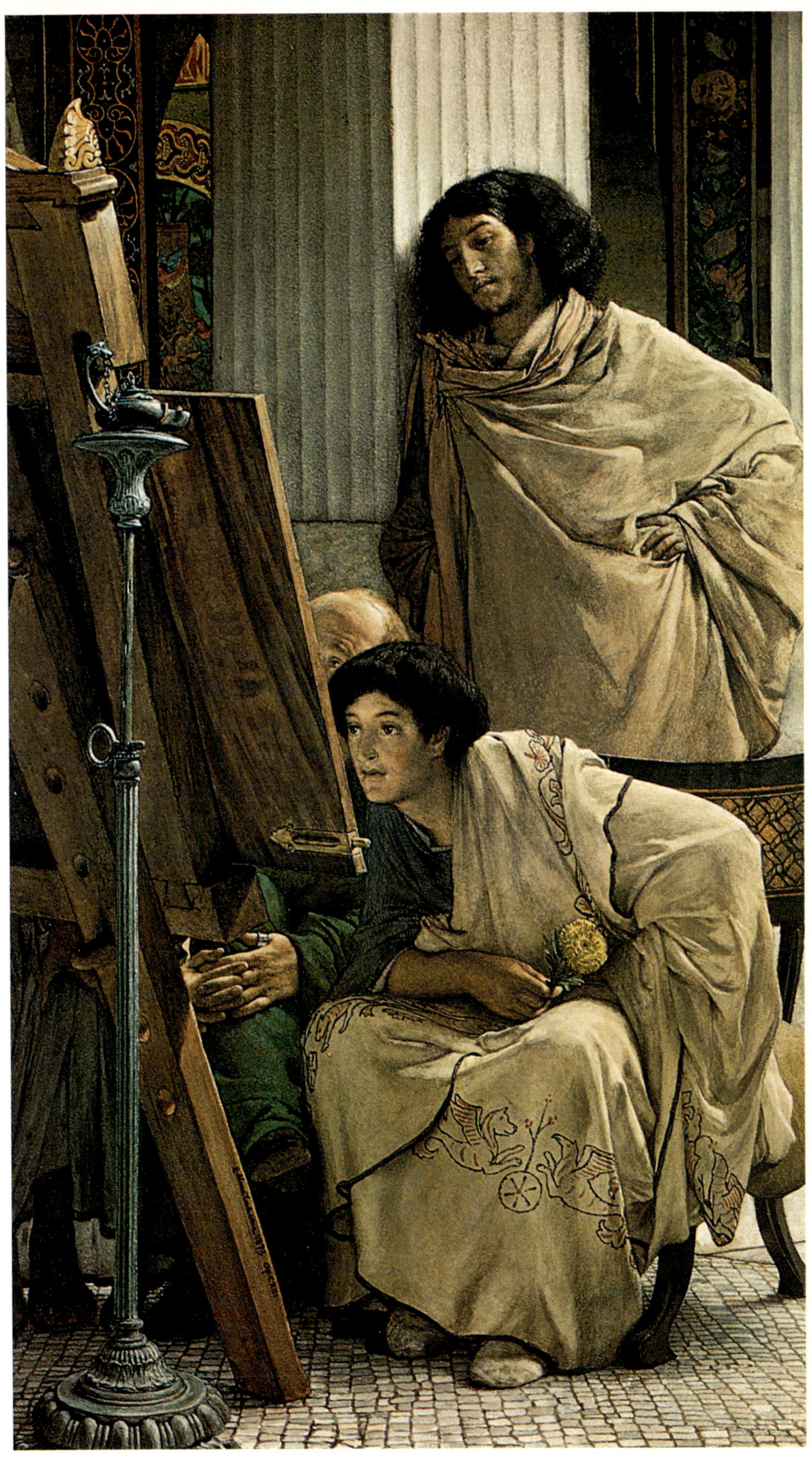

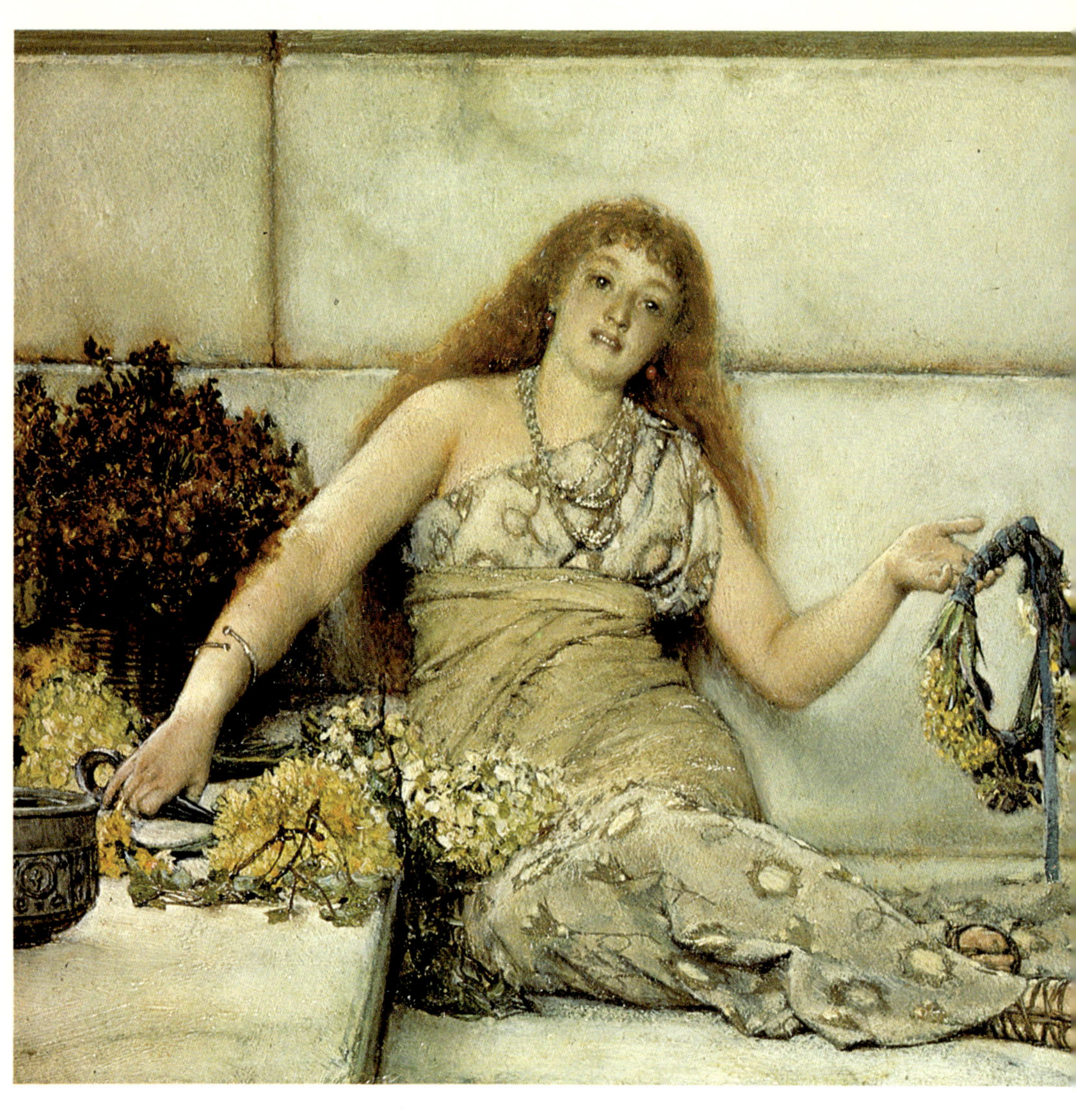

18 *On the steps of the Capitol*
1874 Op CXXXII
9x17 in

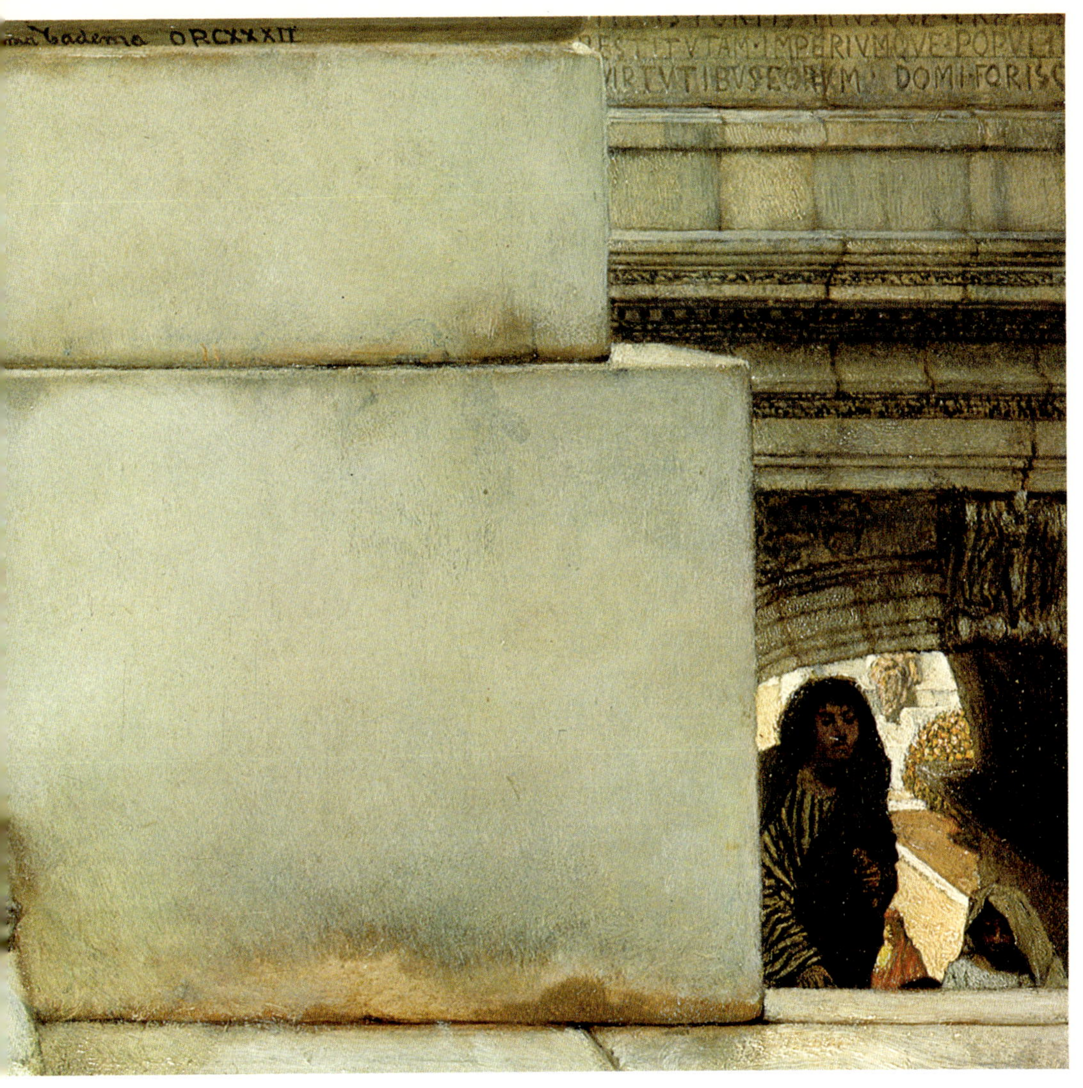

19

Between Hope and Fear
1876 Op. CLXIII
30¾x50½ in

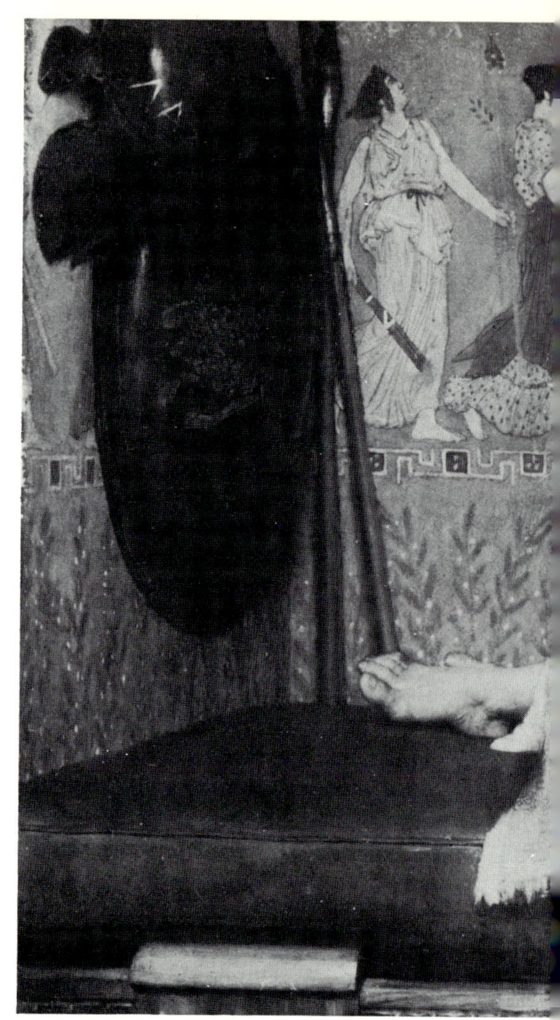

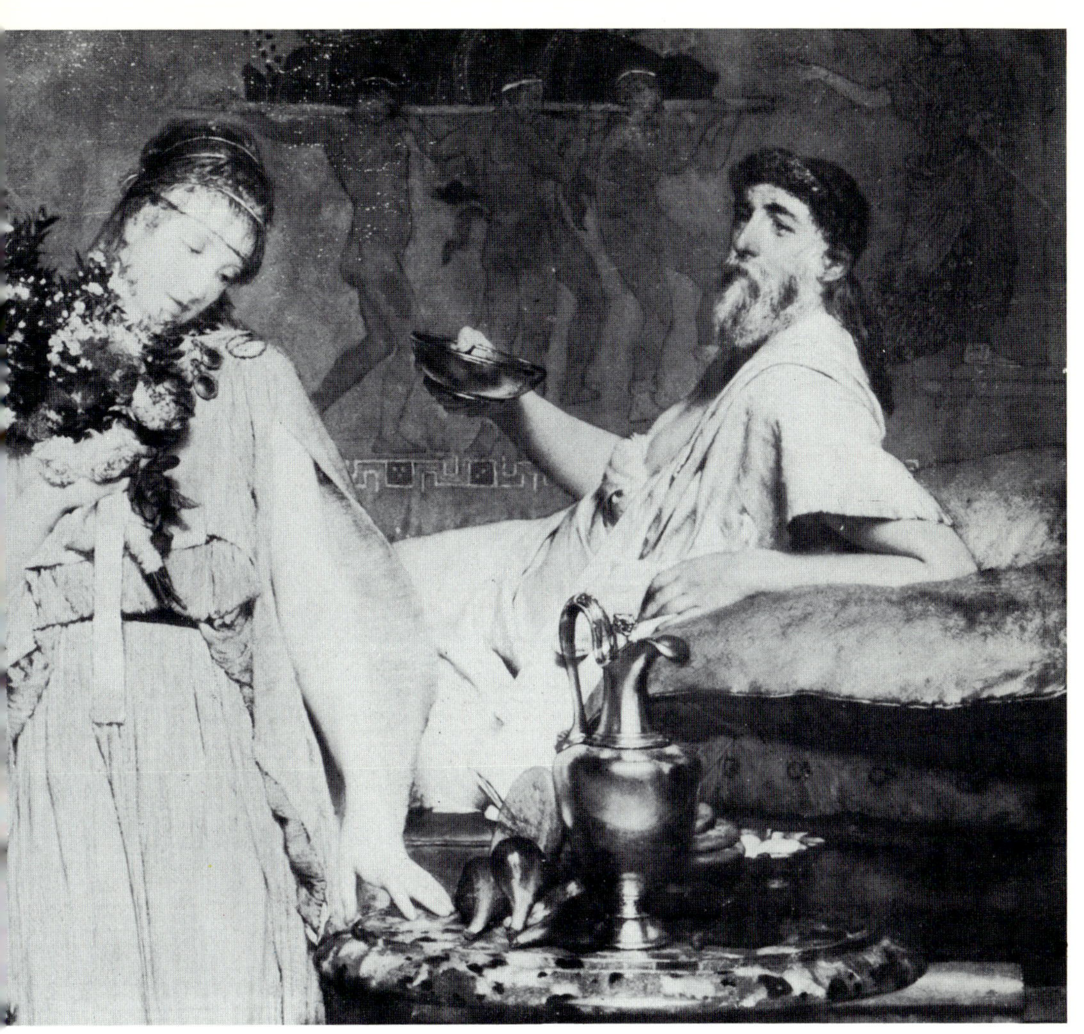

20

Between Hope and Fear
(detail)

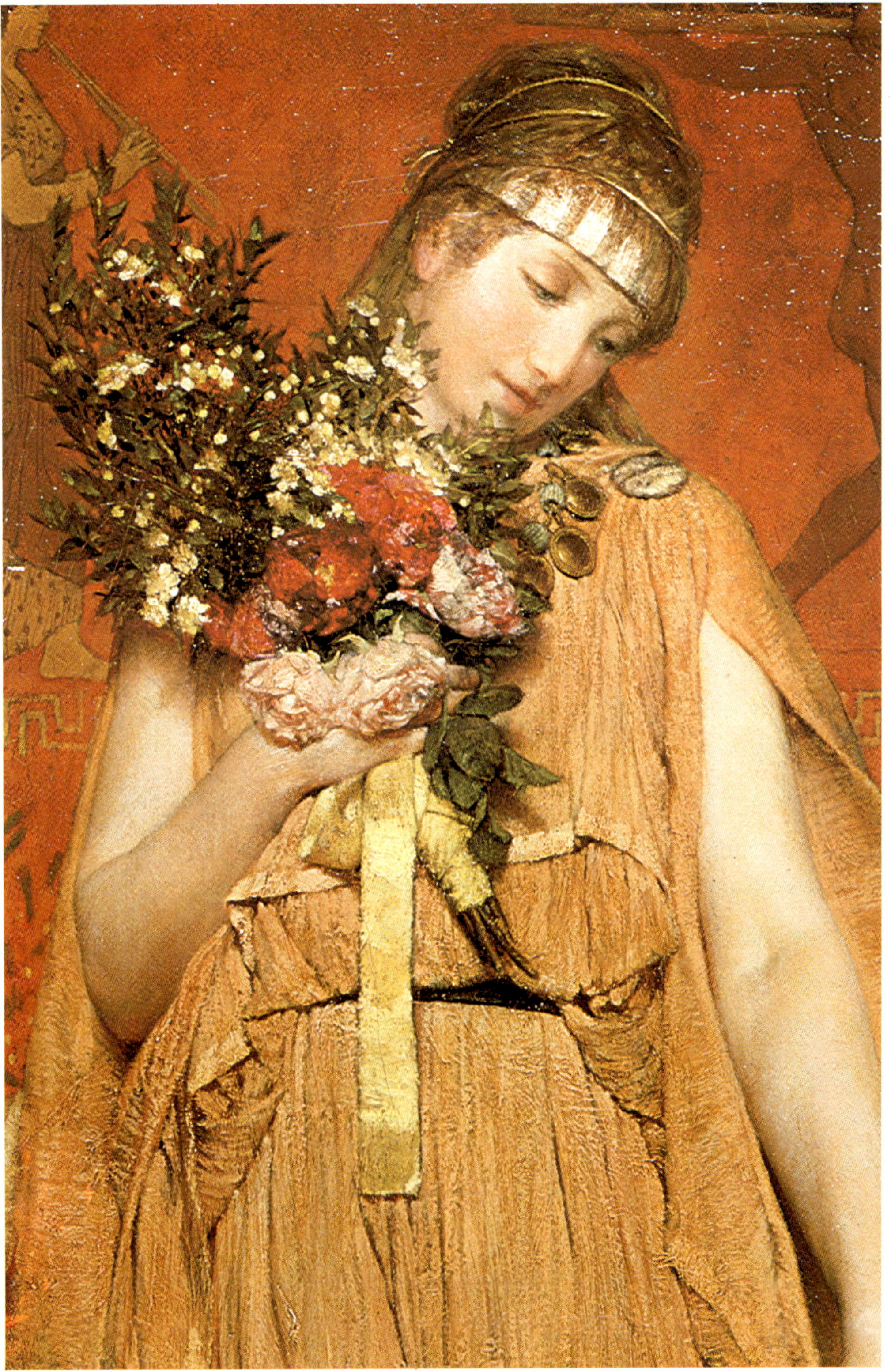

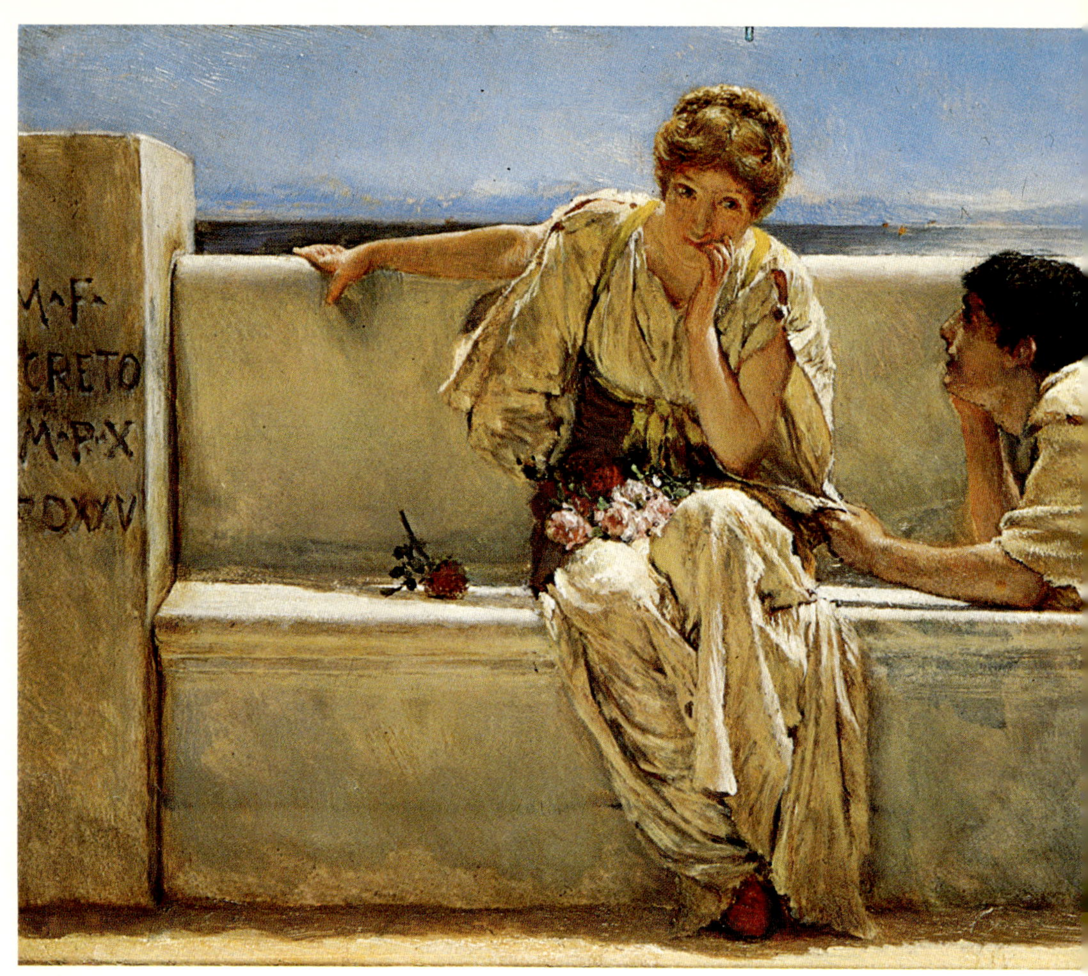

21 *The Question*
1877 Op. CLXXXV
6½×15 in

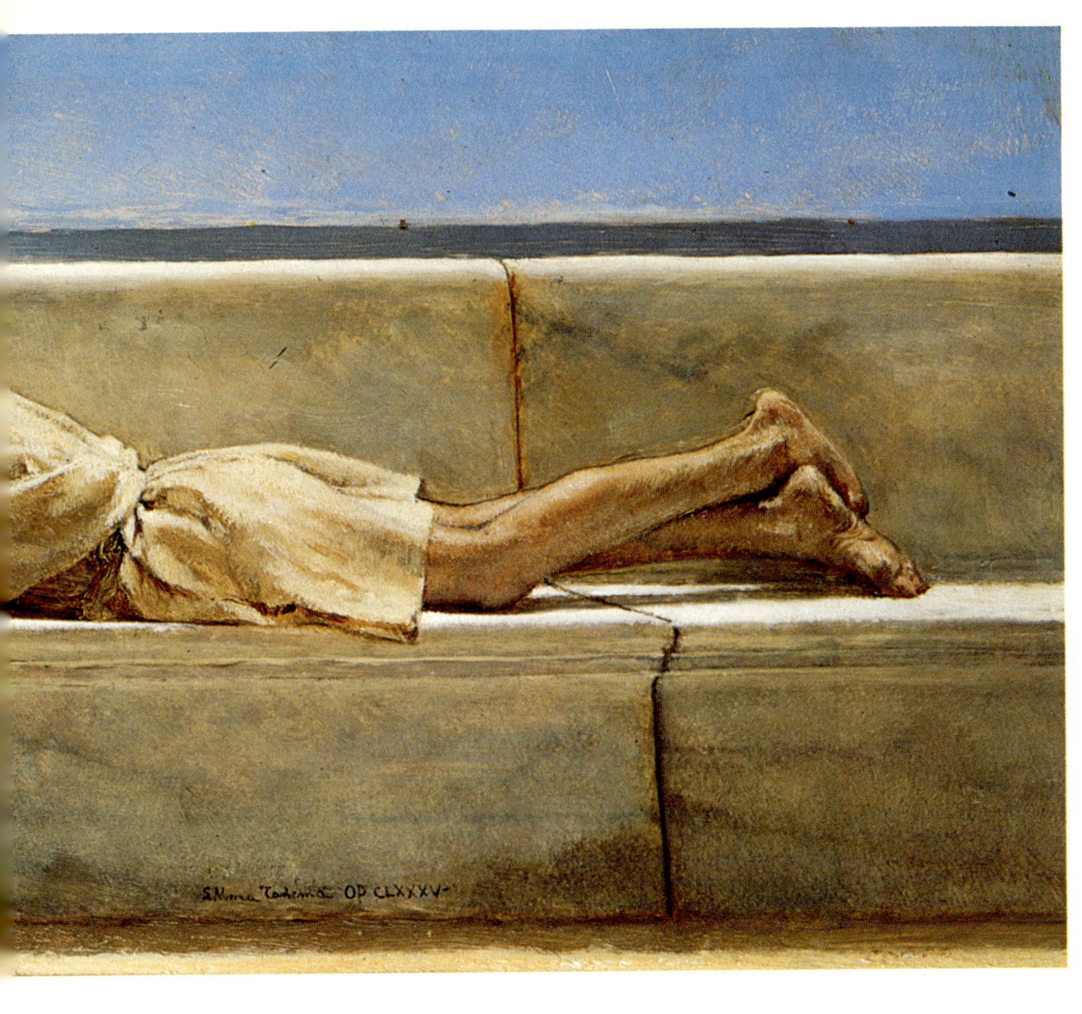
S.Alma Tadema OP CLXXXV

22

An Audience
1881 Op. CCXXVI
9¼x5¾ in

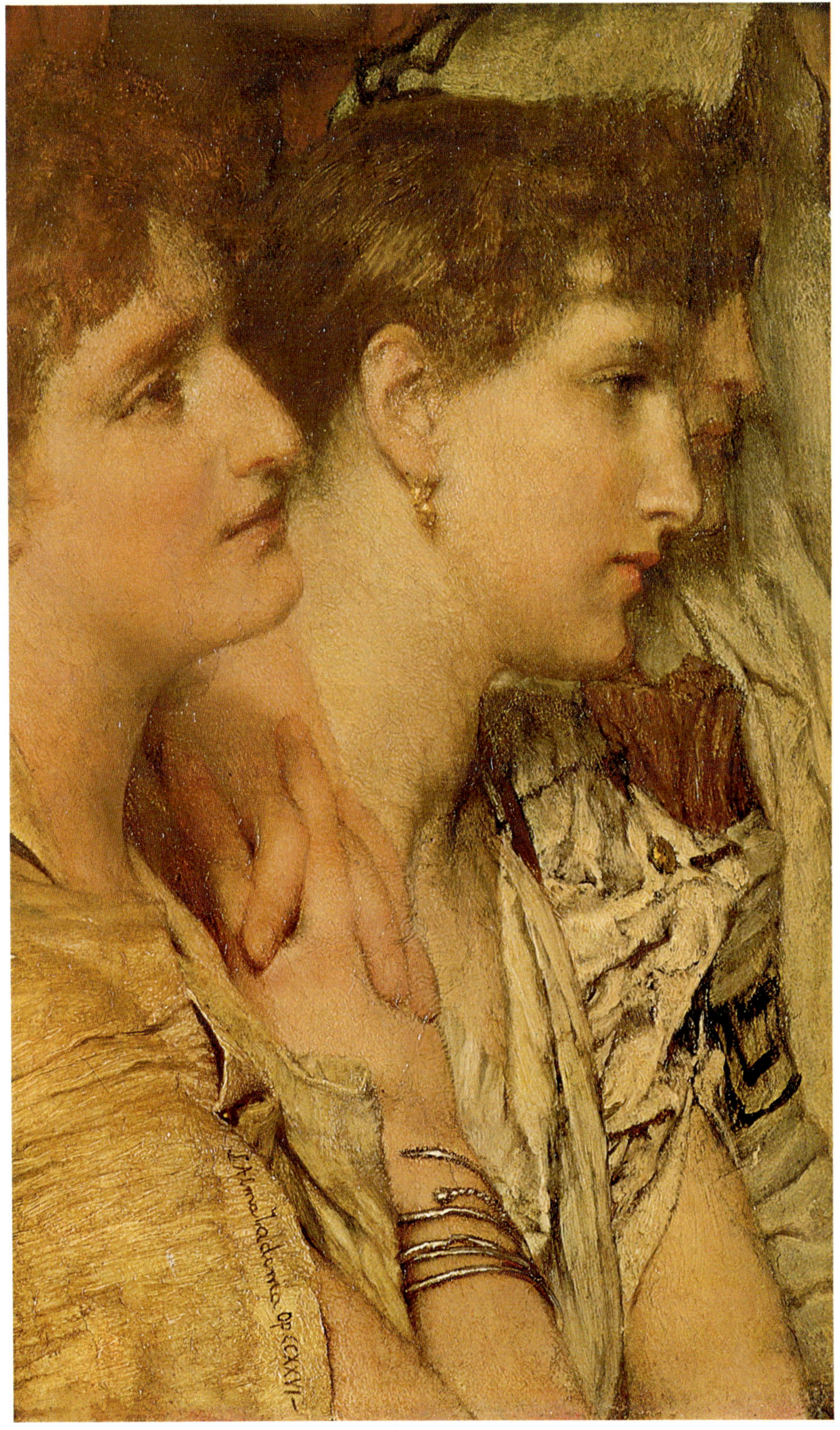
L Alma Tadema Op CCXXVI

23

In the Tepidarium
1881 Op. CCXXIX
9¾x13¼ in

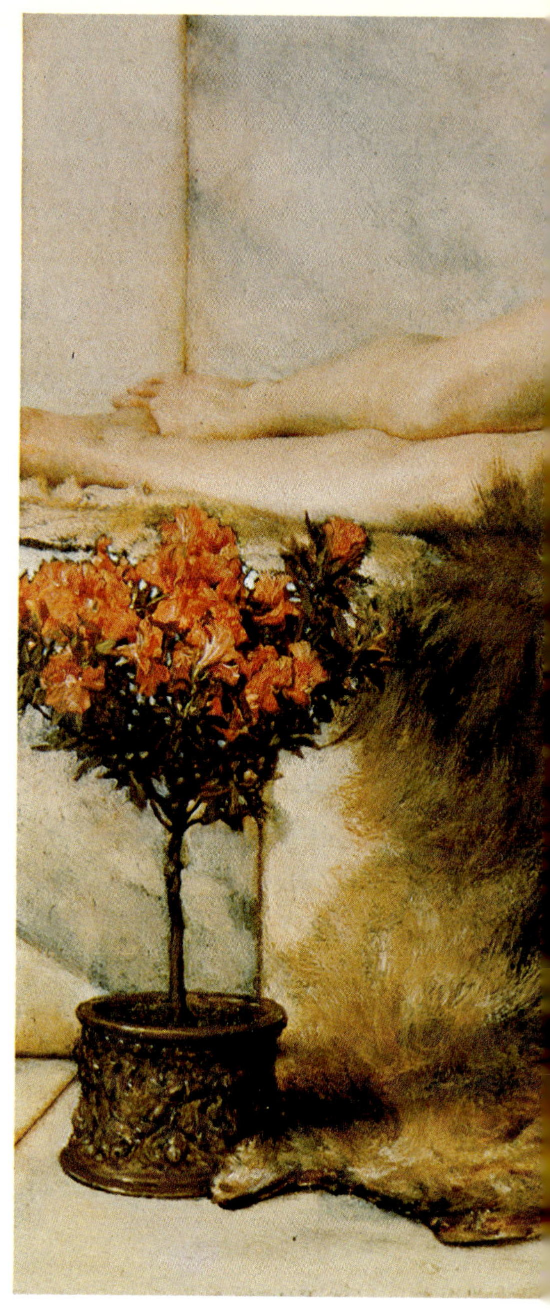

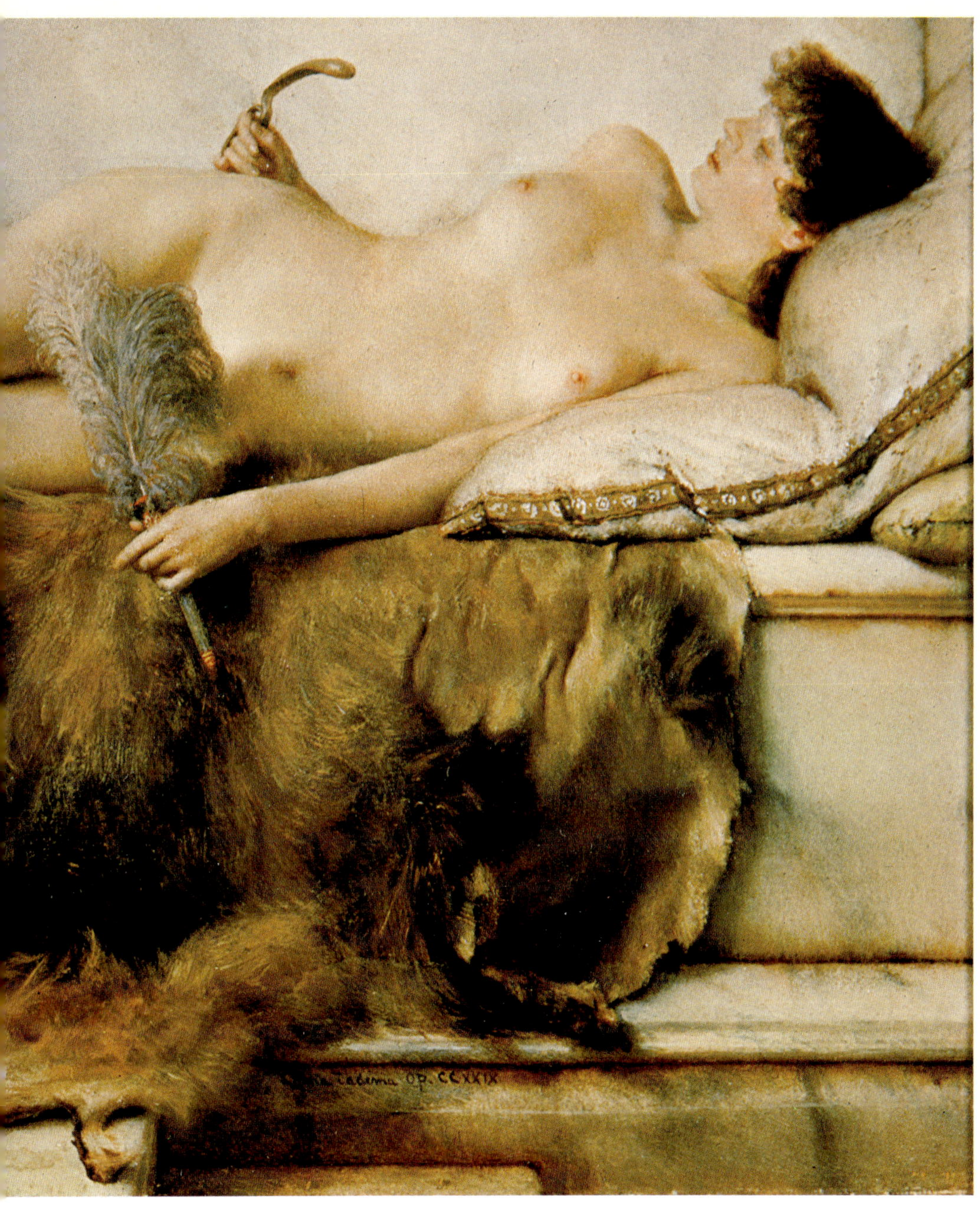

L. Alma Tadema OP. CCXXIX

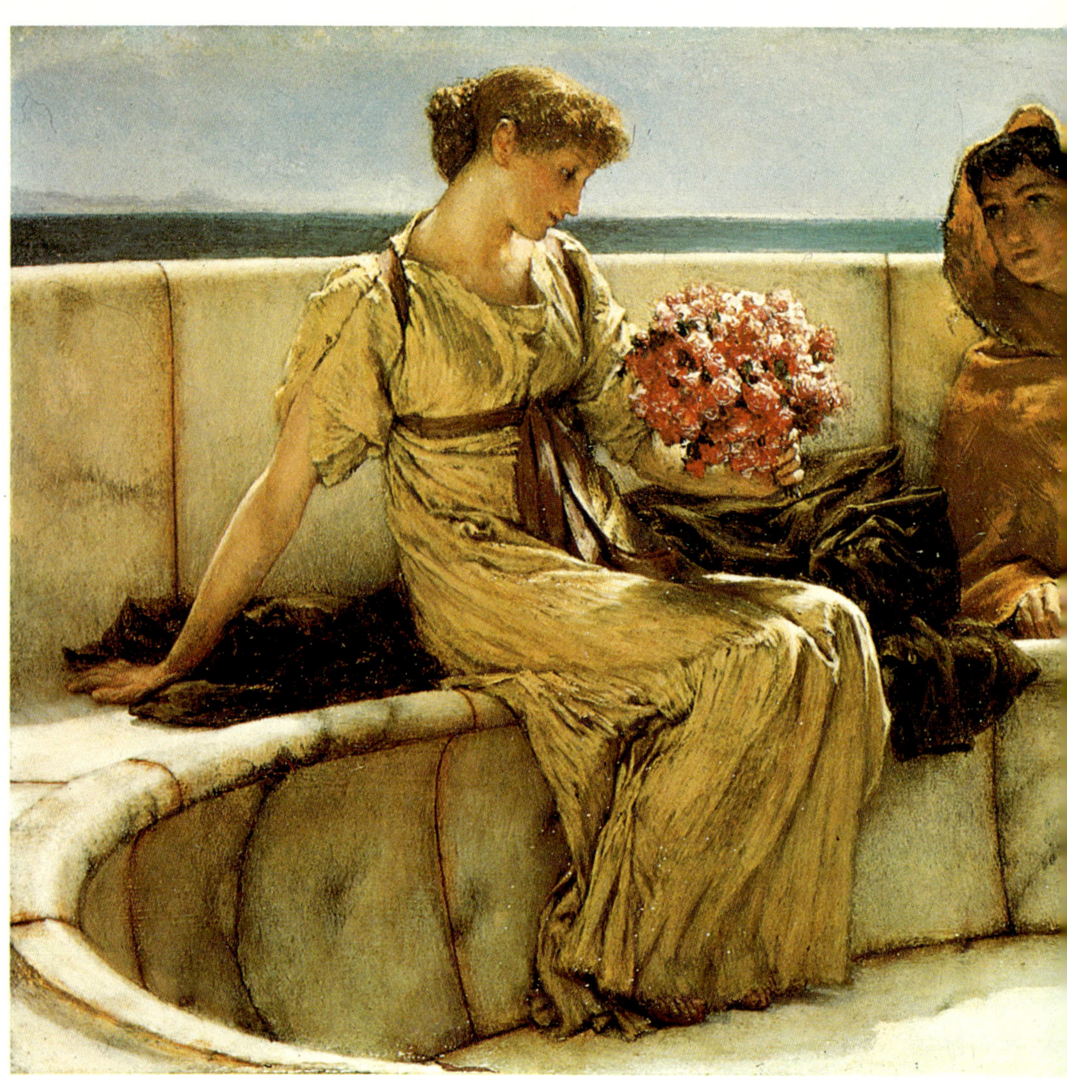

24 *Amo te, ama me*
1881 Op. CCXXXIV
6¾x15 in

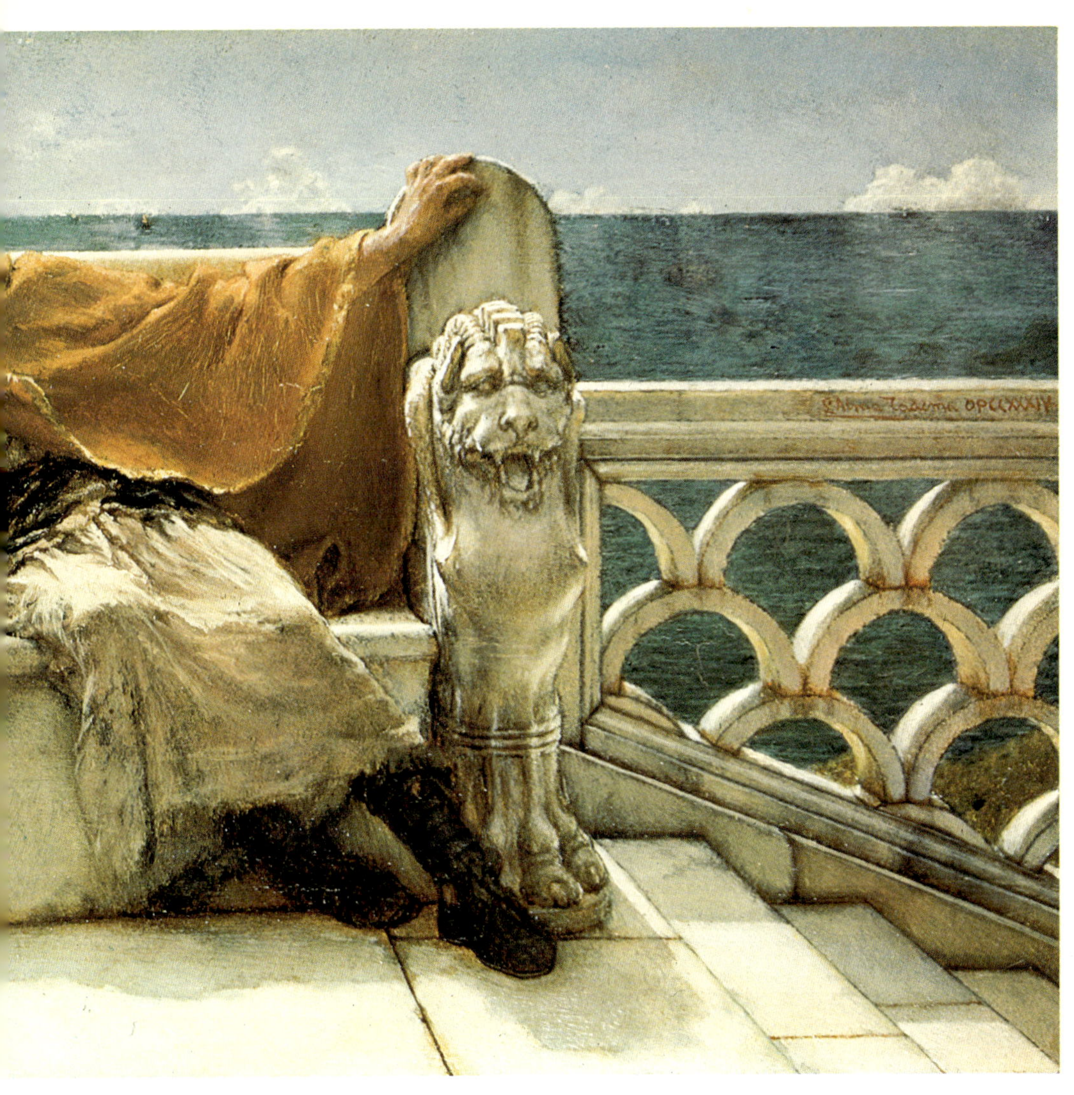

25

The Parting Kiss
1882 Op. CCXL
44½x29 in

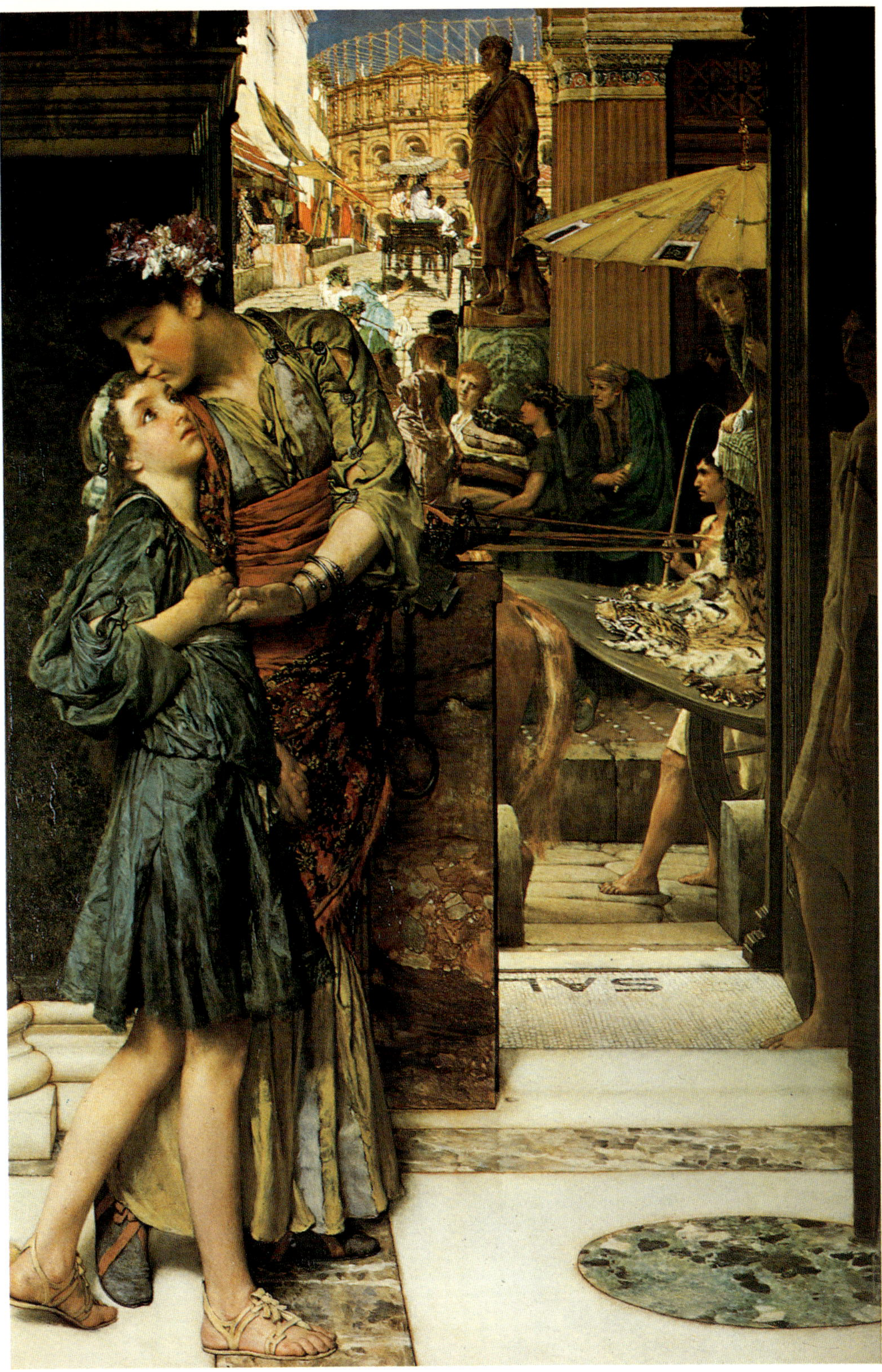

26

The Oleander
1882 Op. CCXLV
36½x25¾ in

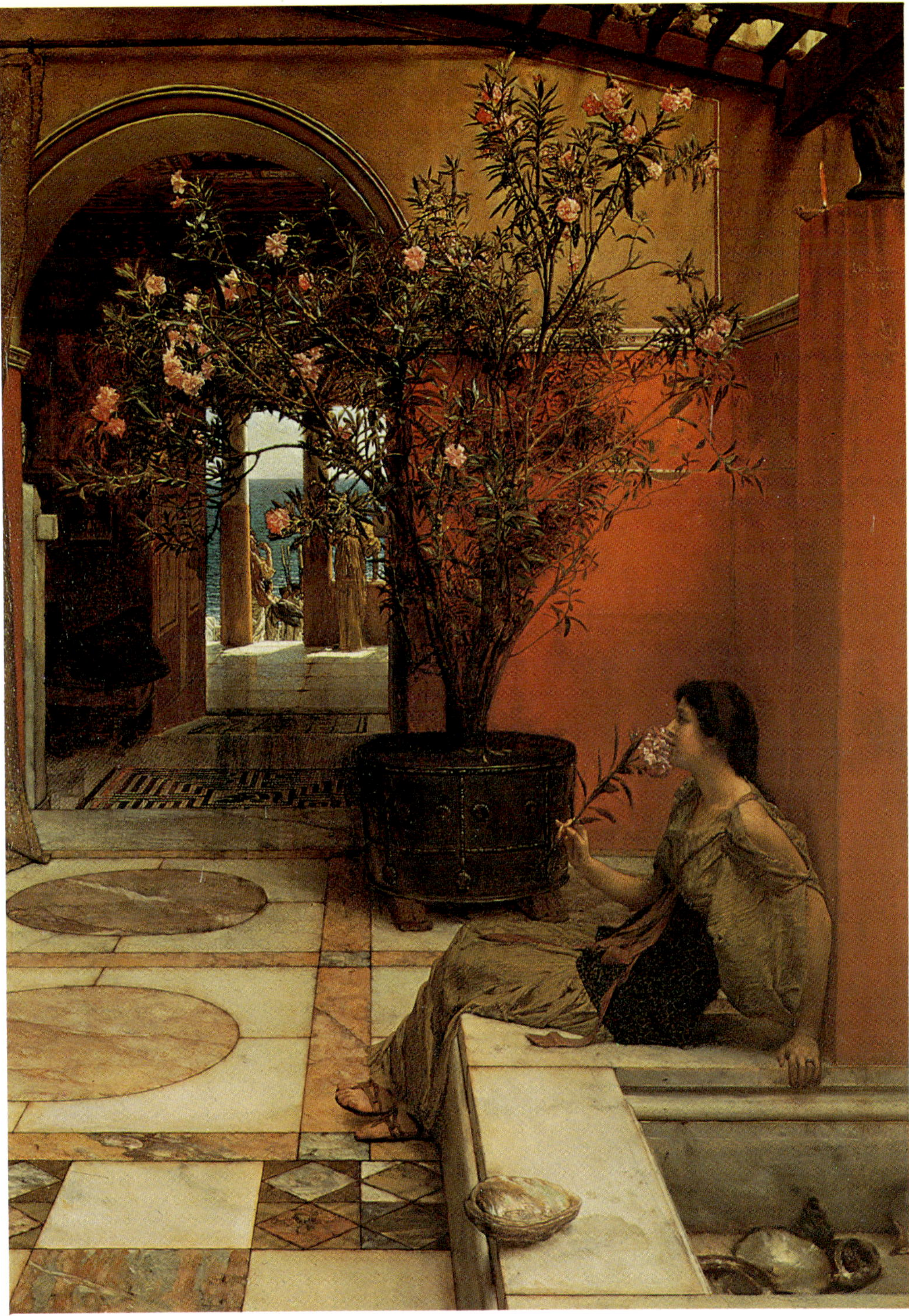

27

Anthony and Cleopatra
1883 Op. CCXLVI
25¾x36¼ in

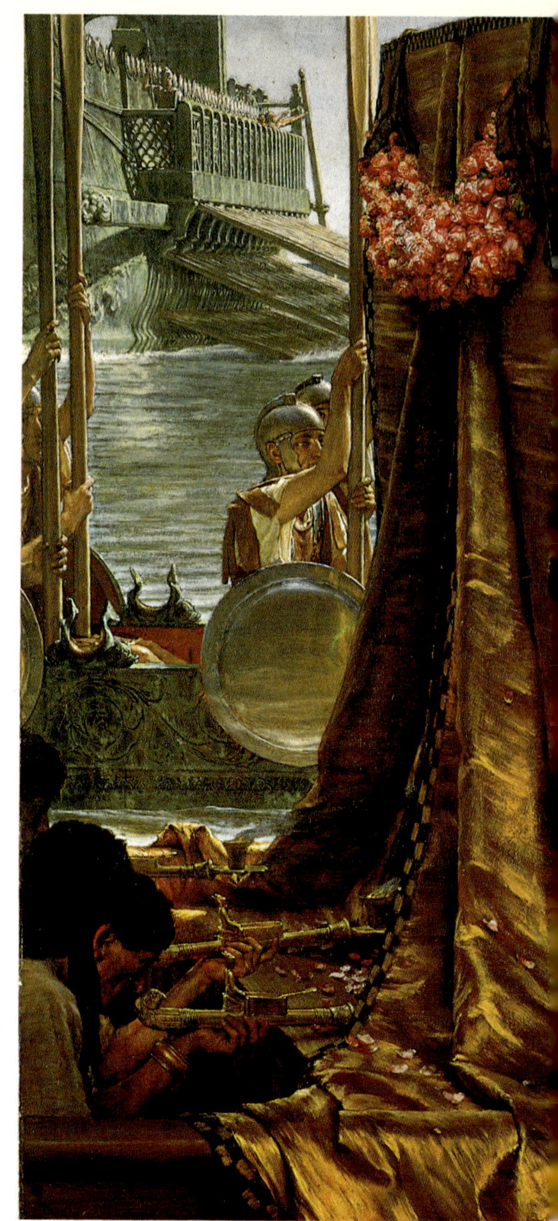

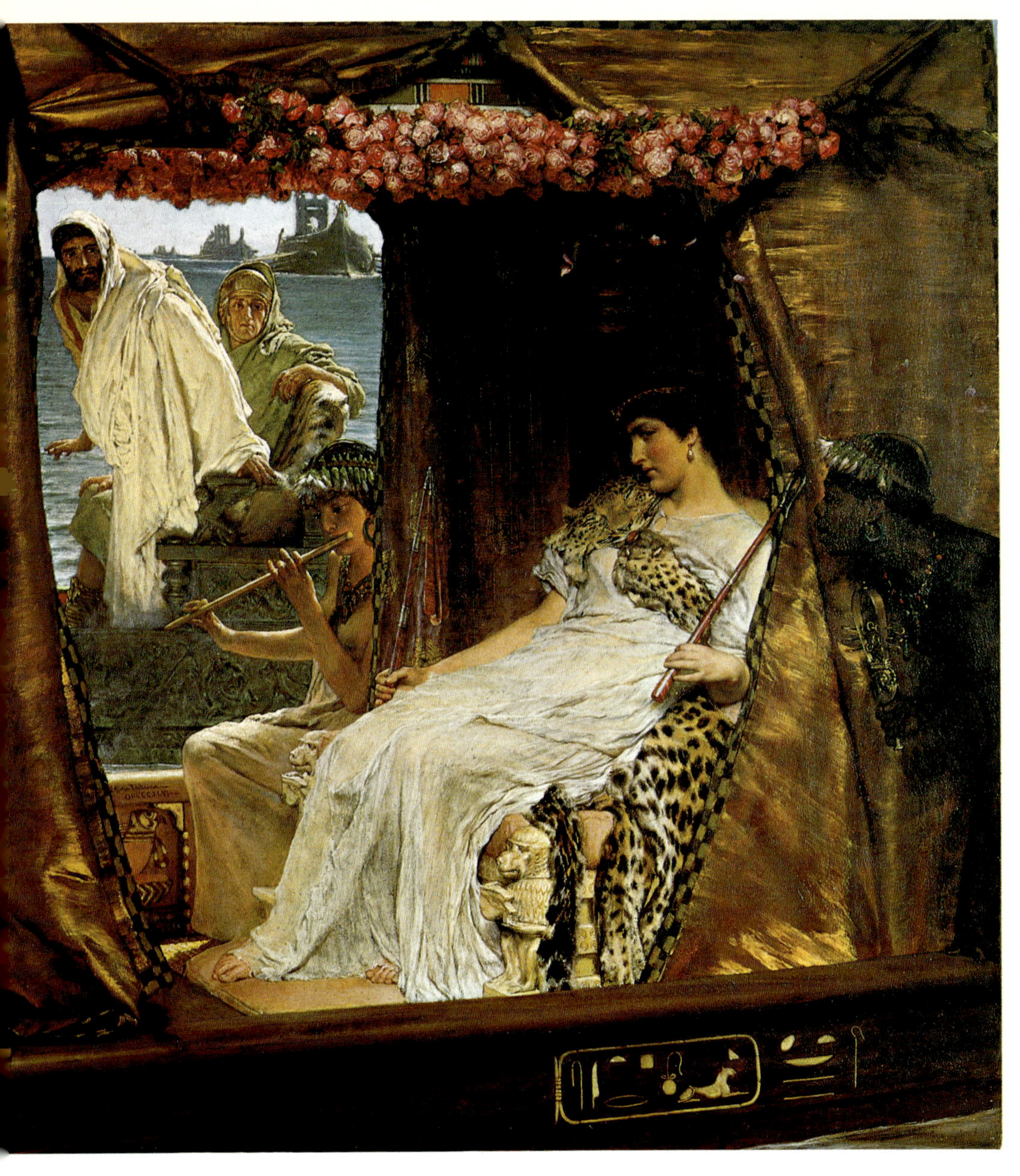

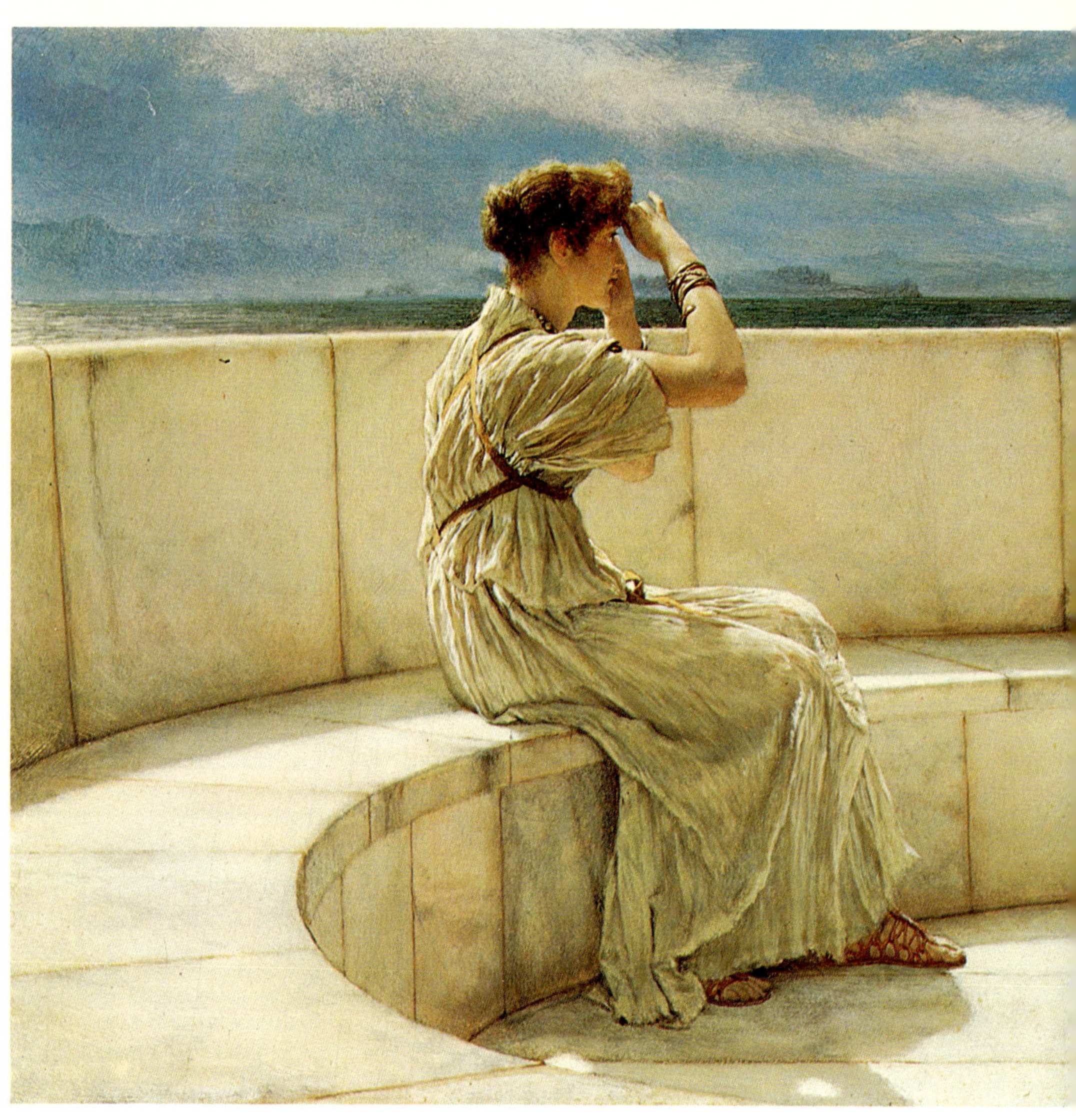

28 *Expectations*
1885 Op. CCLXVI
12¾x22½ in

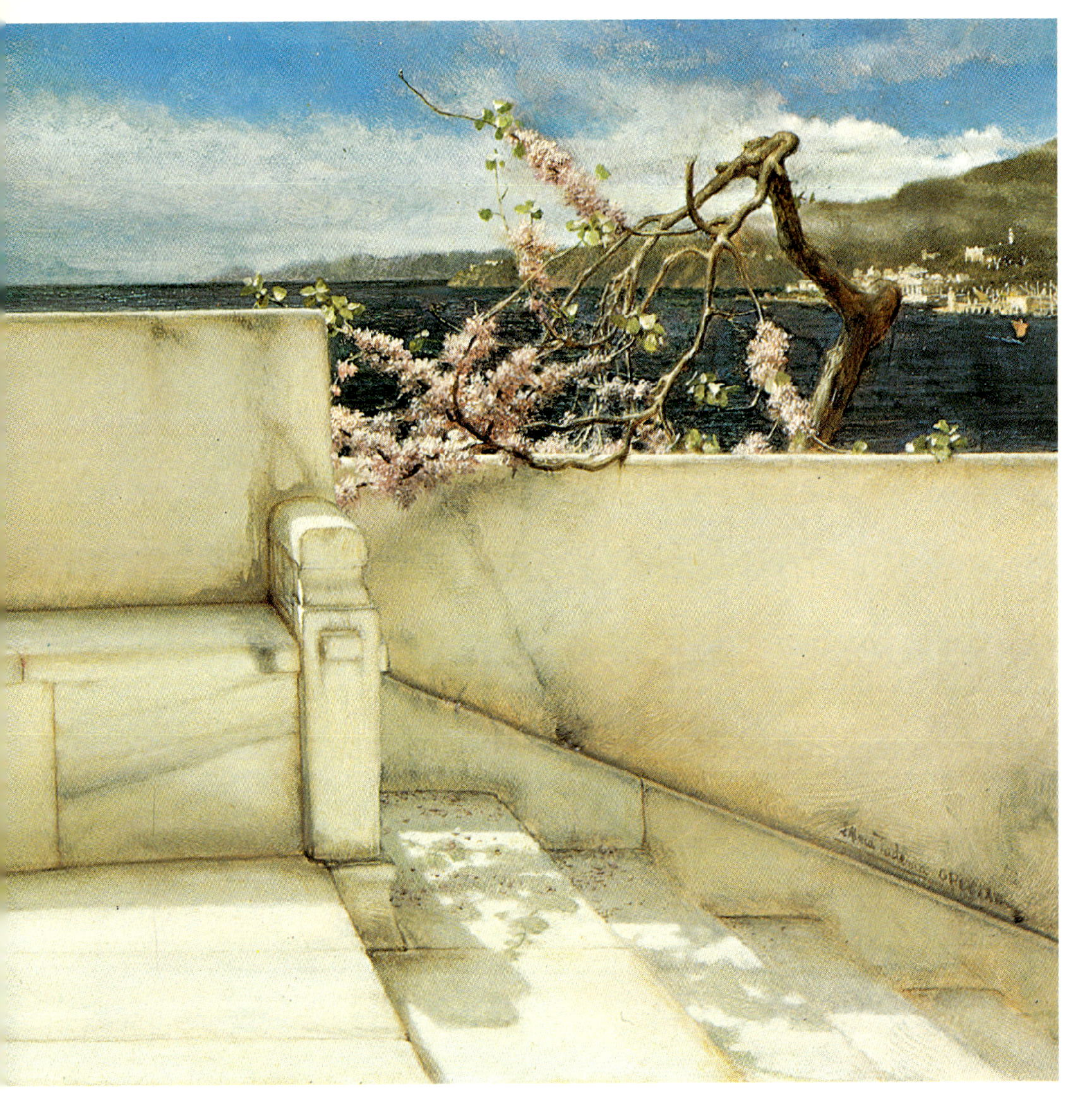

29

The Roses of Heliogabalus
1888 Op. CCLXXXIII
52x84¼ in

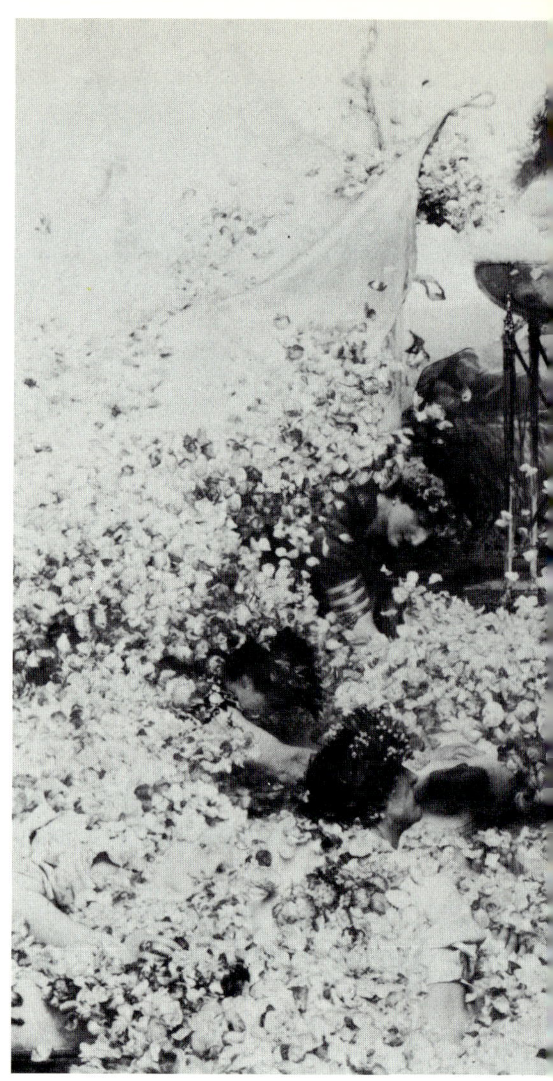

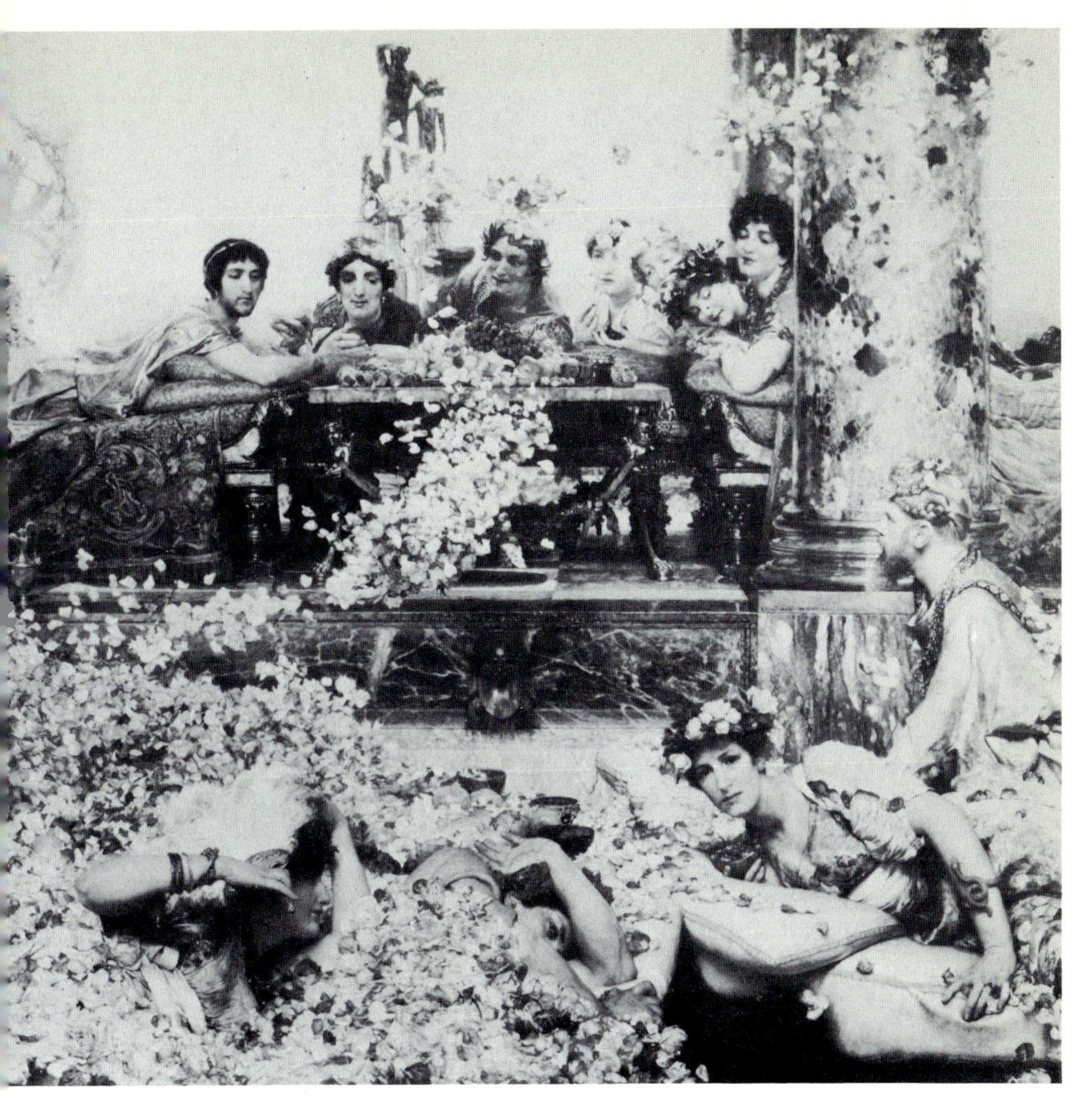

30

The Roses of Heliogabalus
(detail)

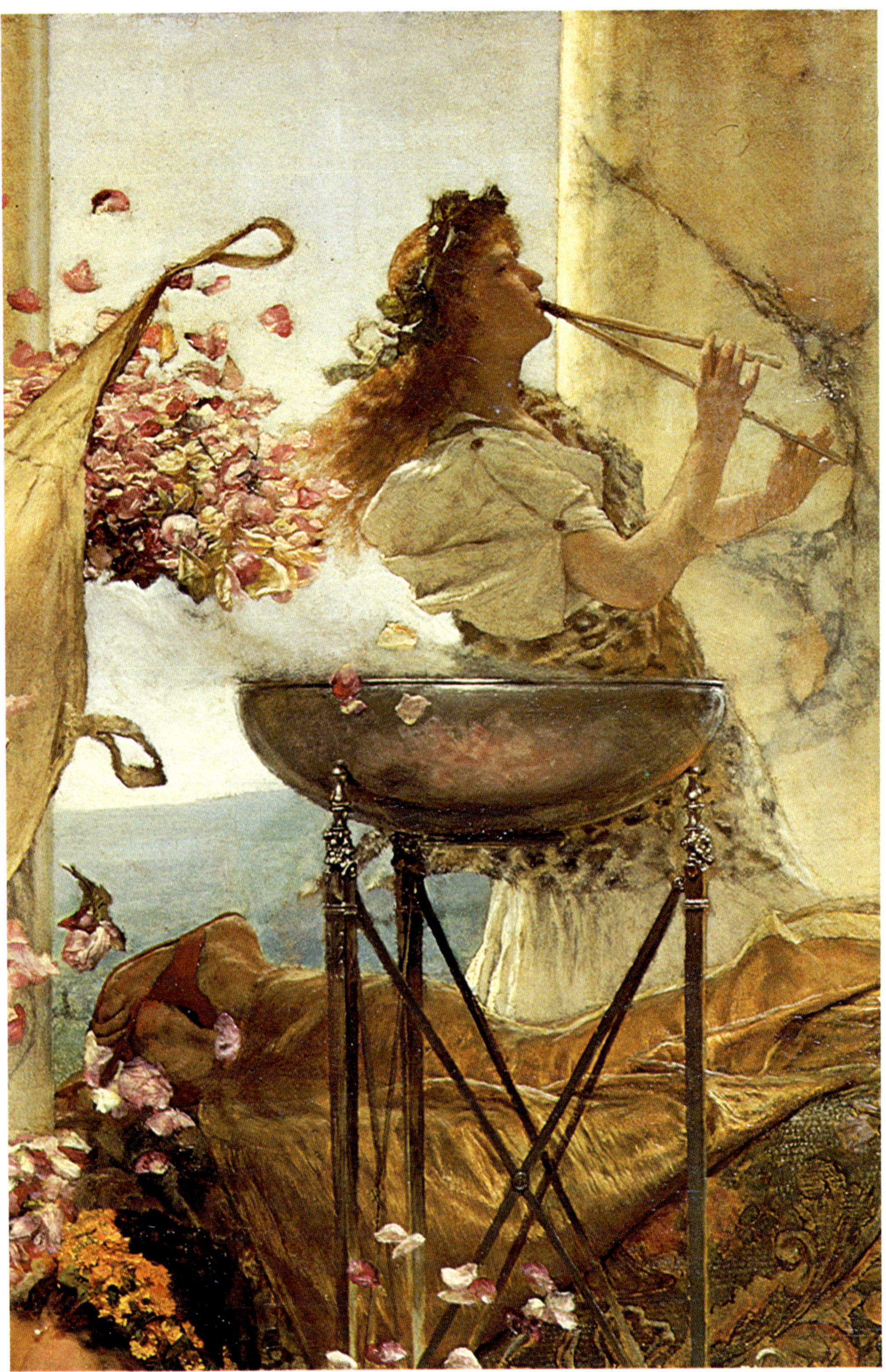

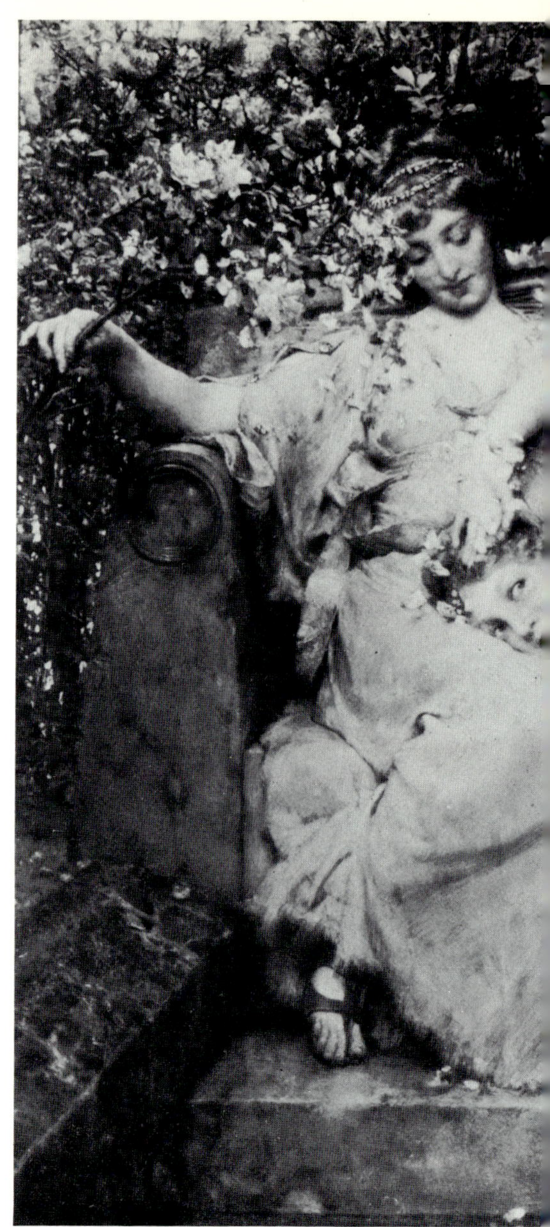

31

In a Rose Garden
1889 Op. CCXCVIII
14¾x20 in

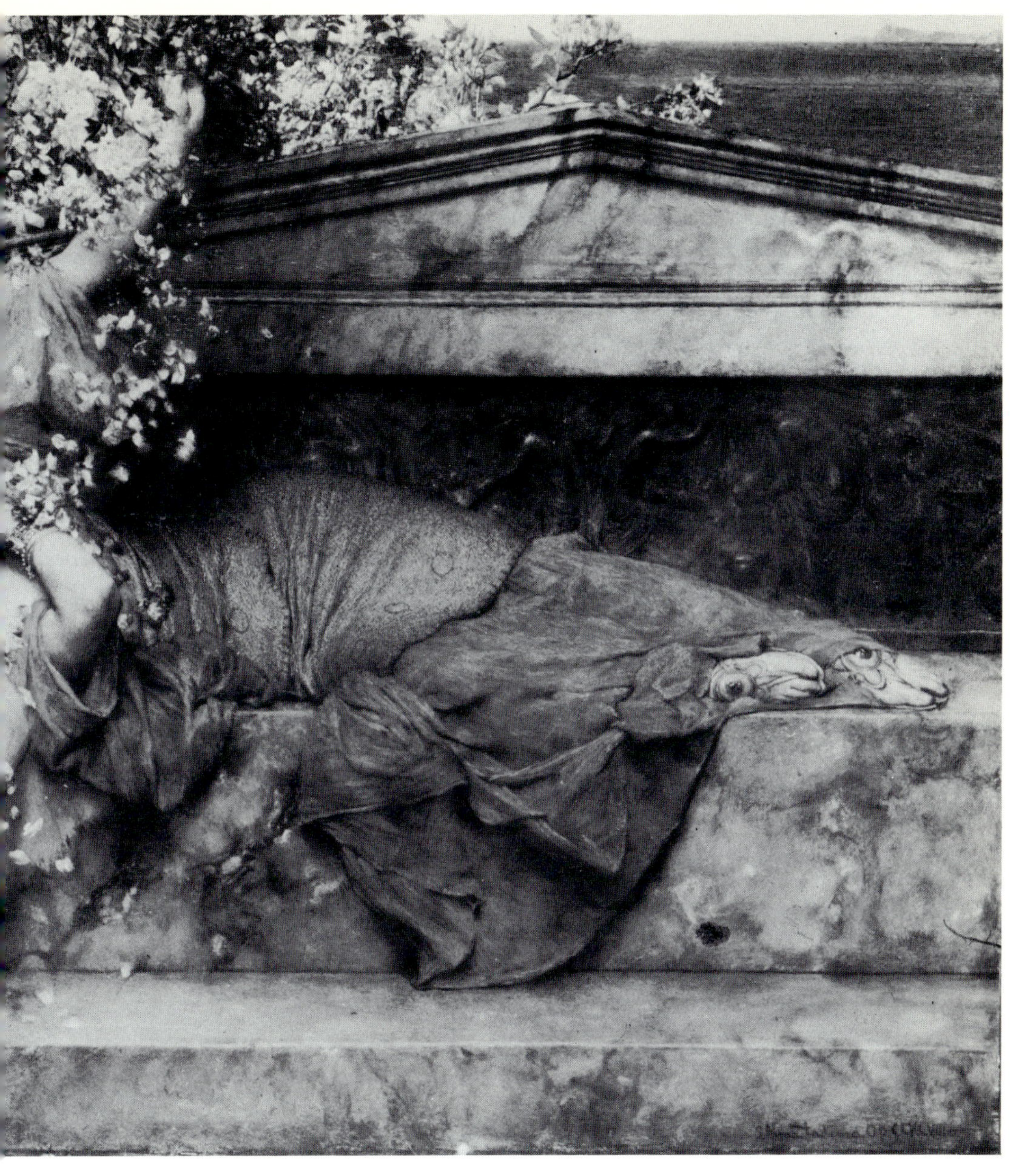

32

In a Rose Garden
(detail)

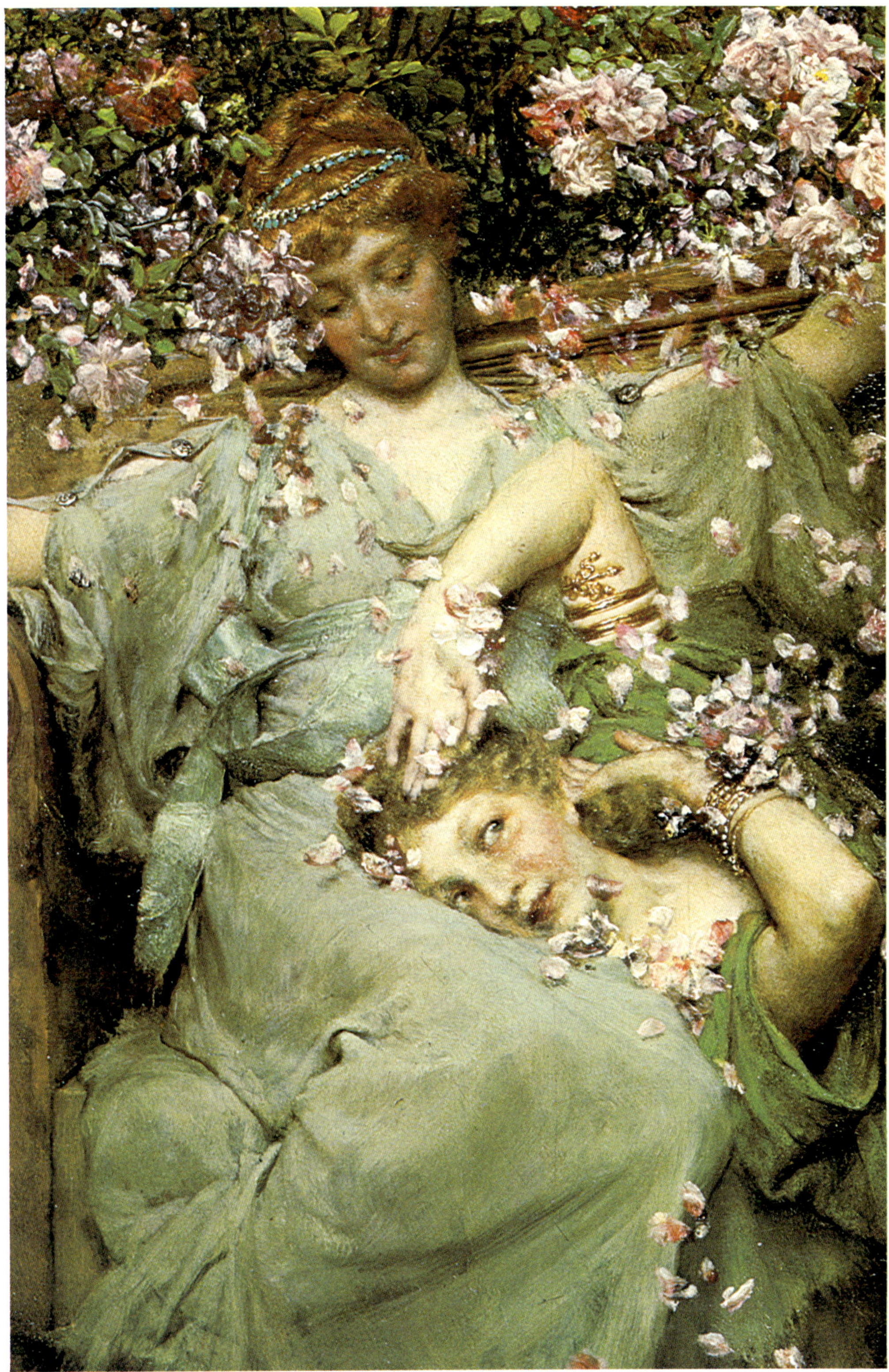

33

The Frigidarium
1890 Op. CCCII
17¾x24 in

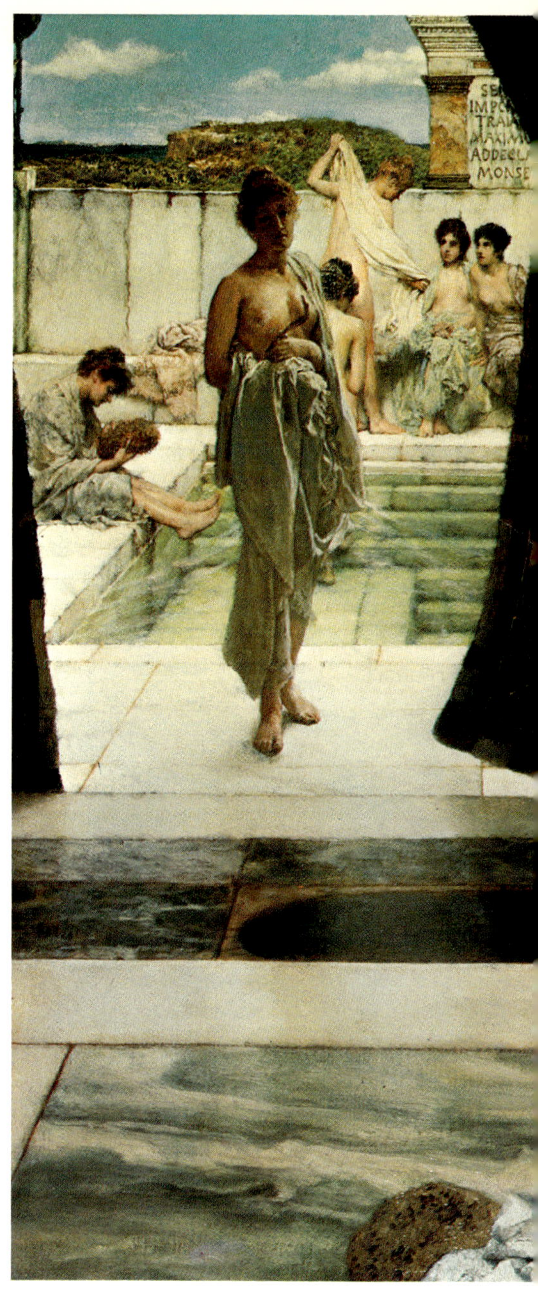

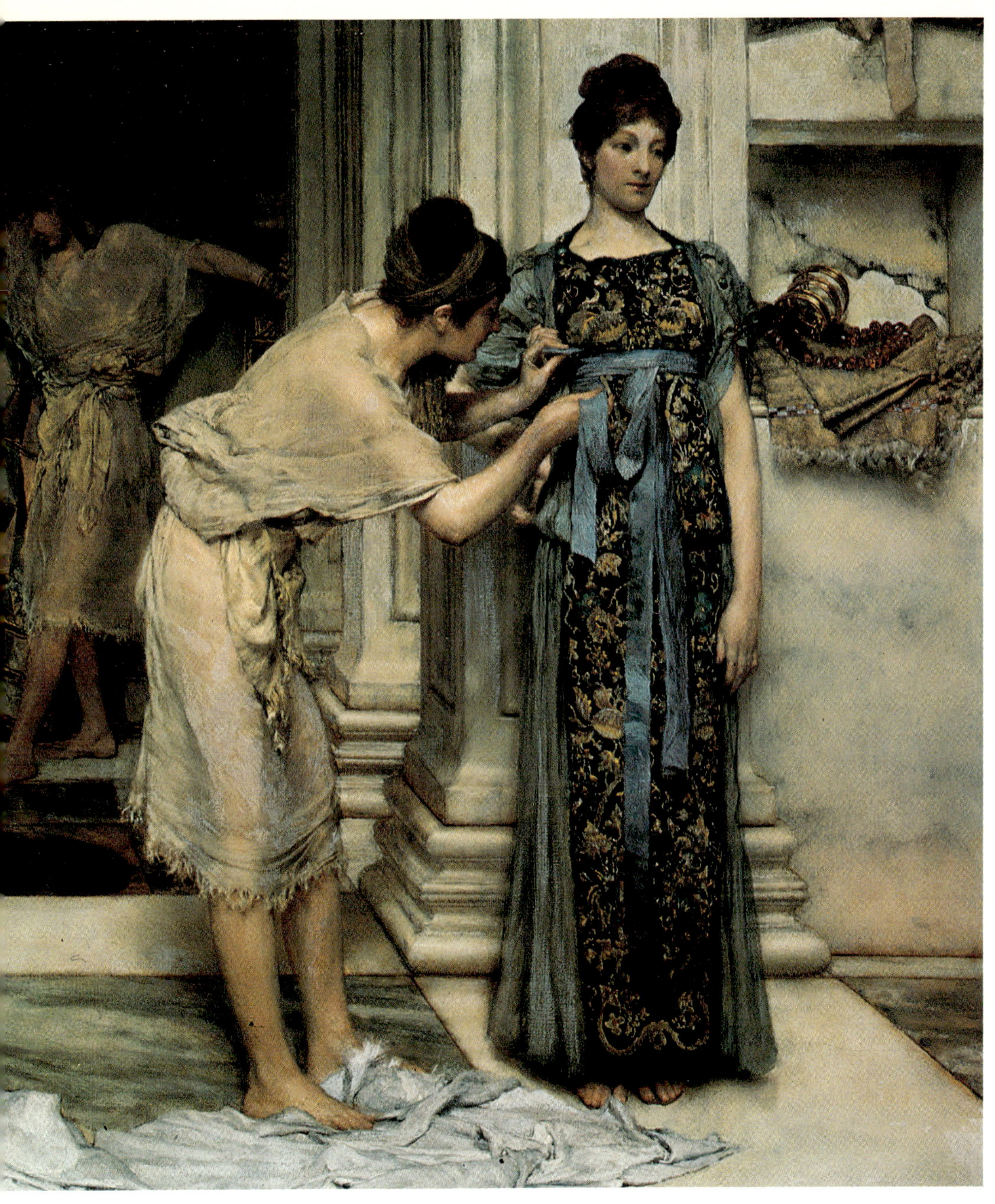

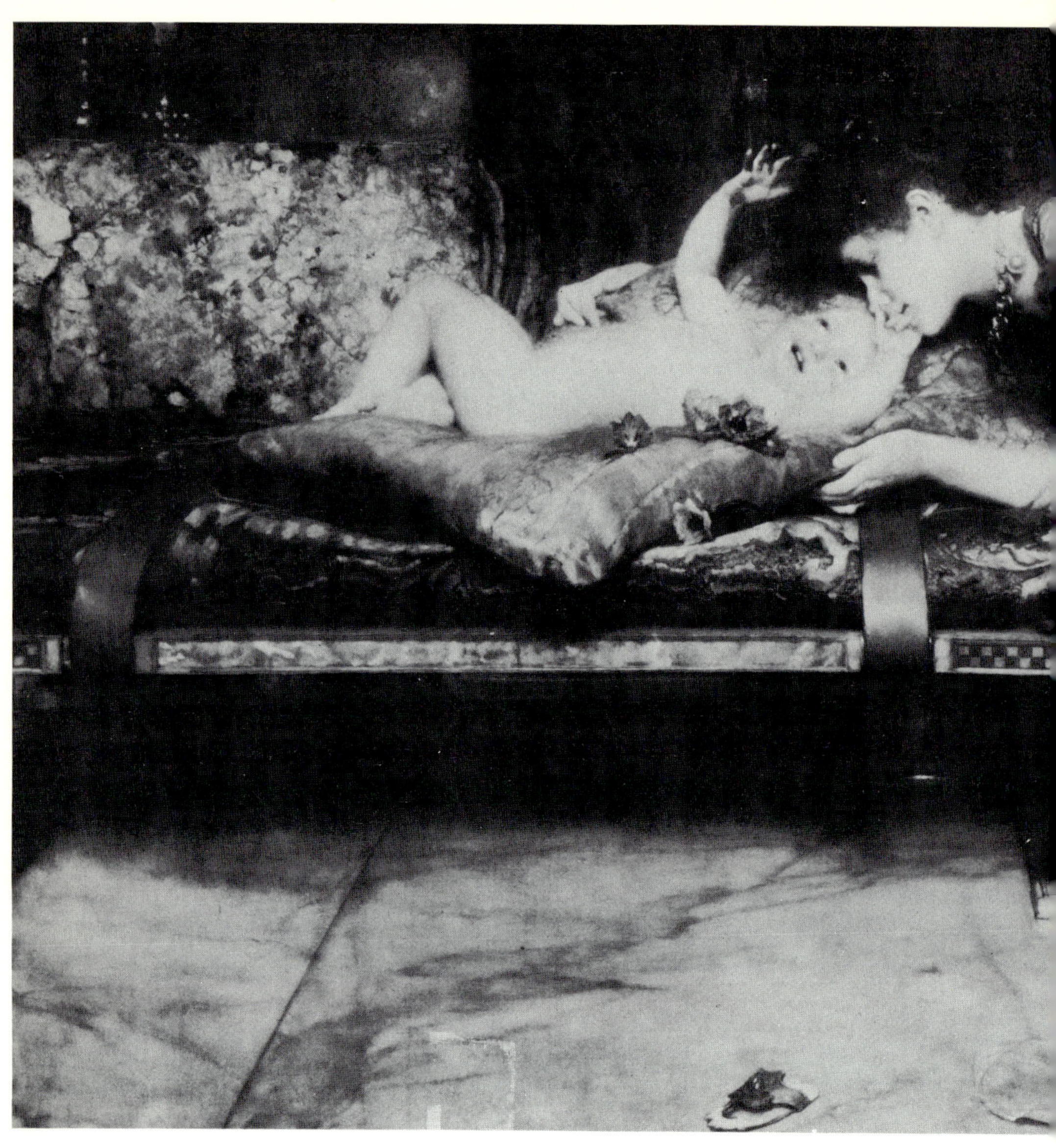

34 *An Earthly Paradise*
1891 Op. CCCVII
34 x 65 in

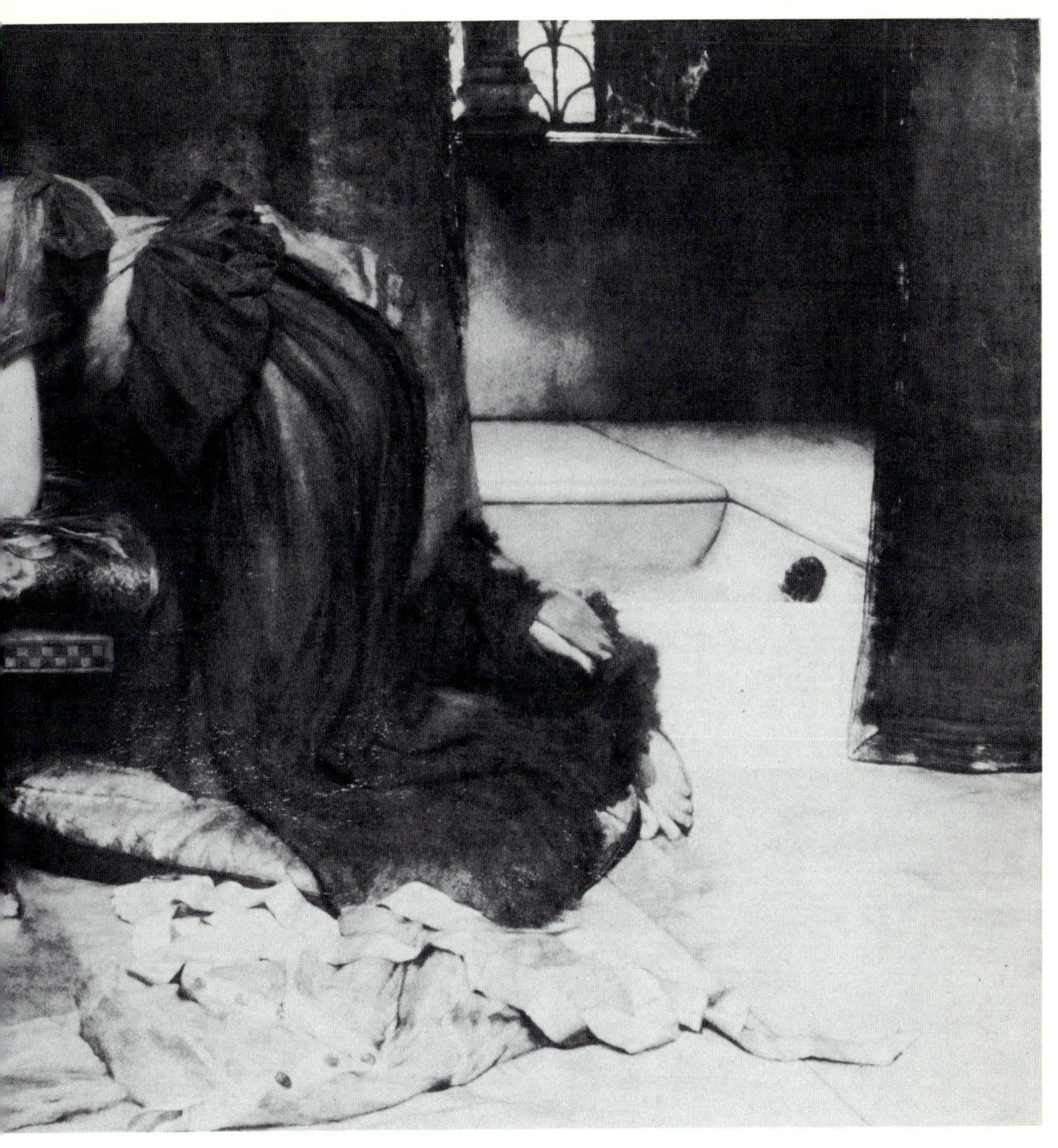

35

An Earthly Paradise
(detail)

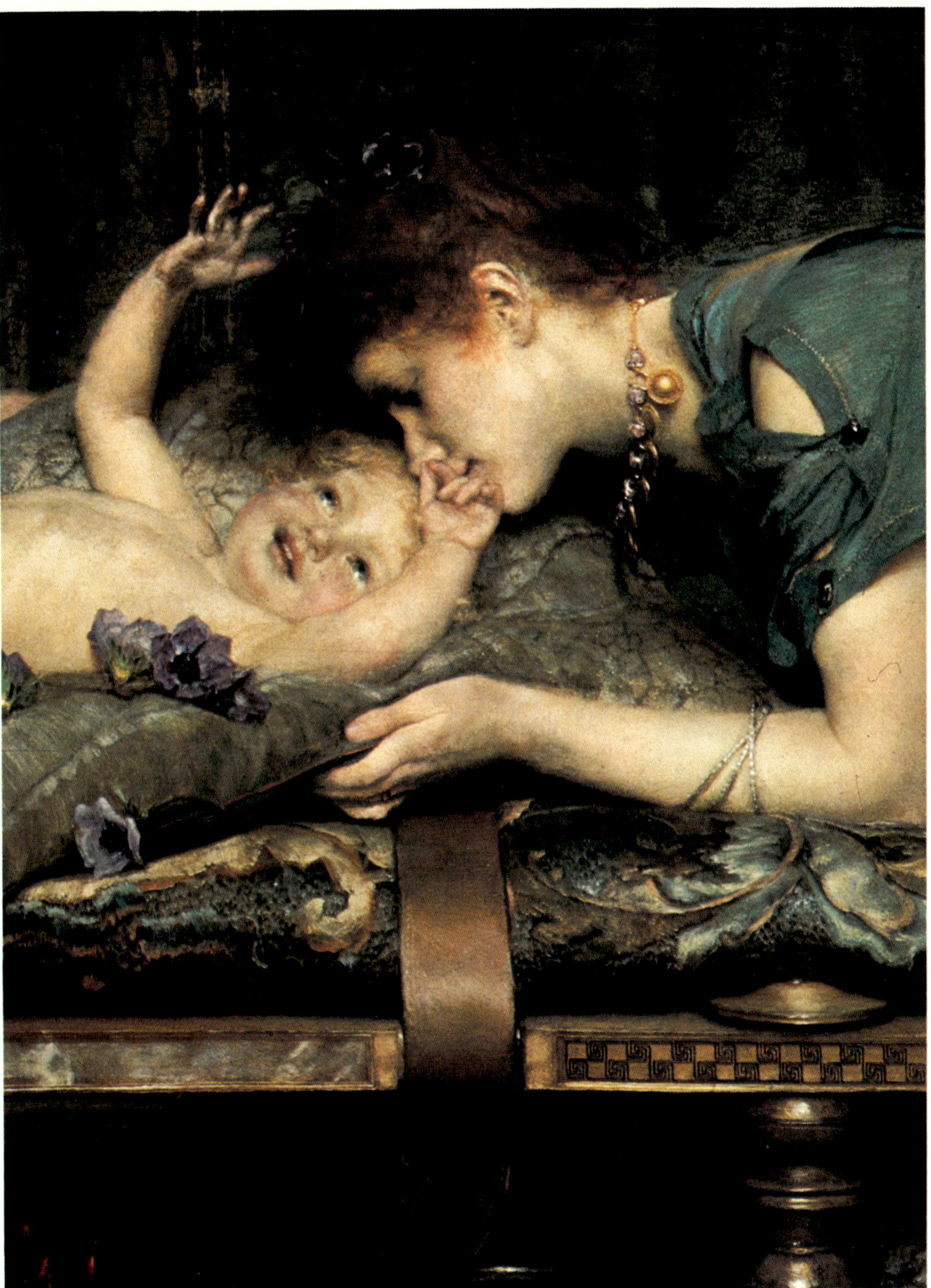

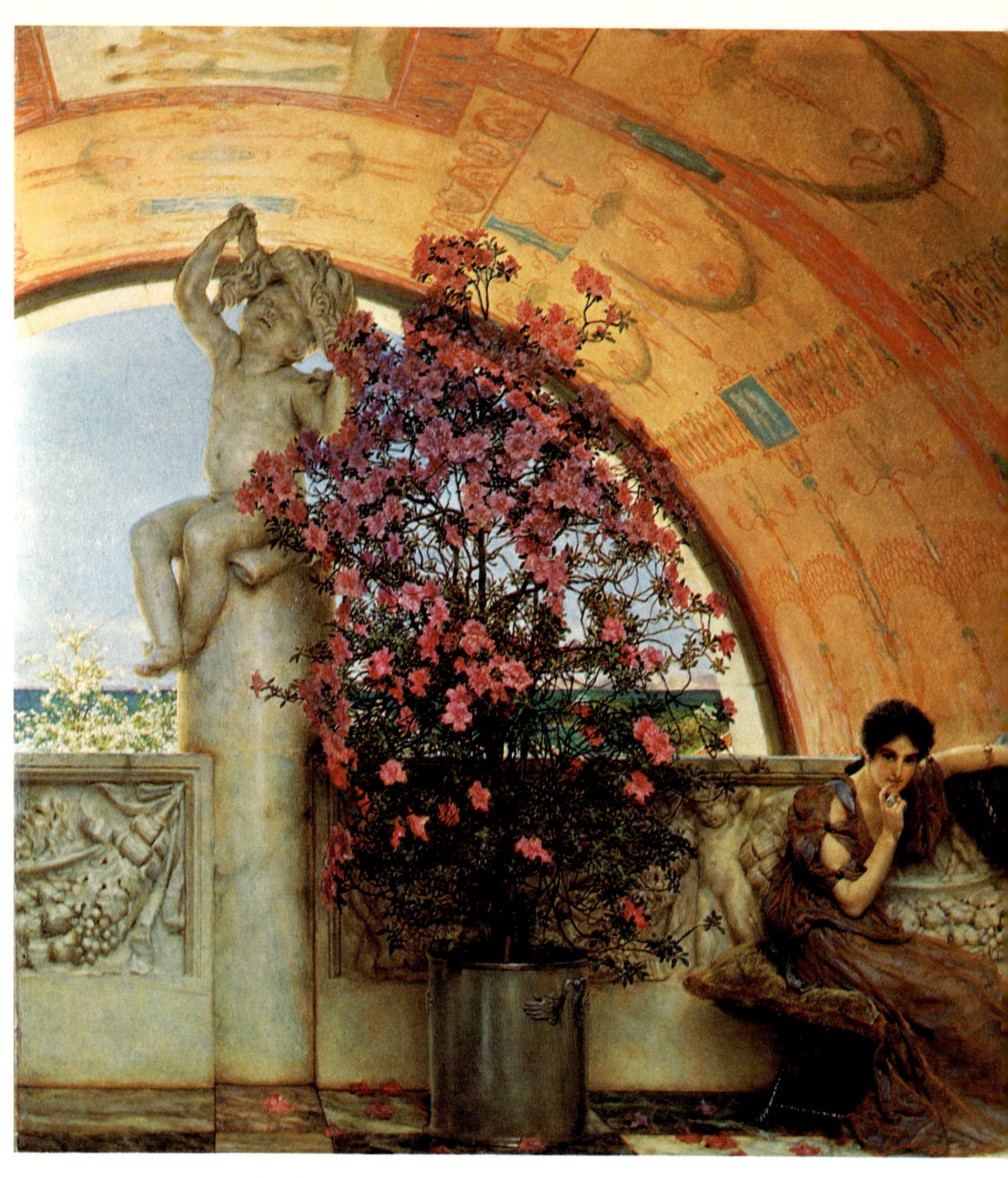

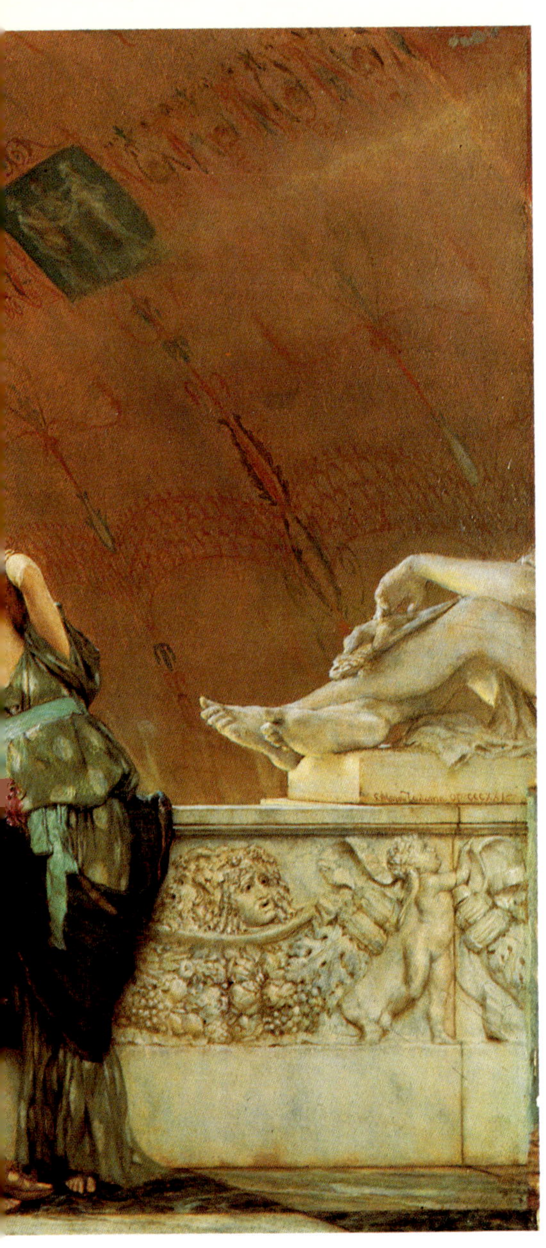

36

Unconscious Rivals
1893 Op. CCCXXI
18x25½ in

37

A Coign of Vantage
1895 Op. CCCXXXIII
25¼x17½ in

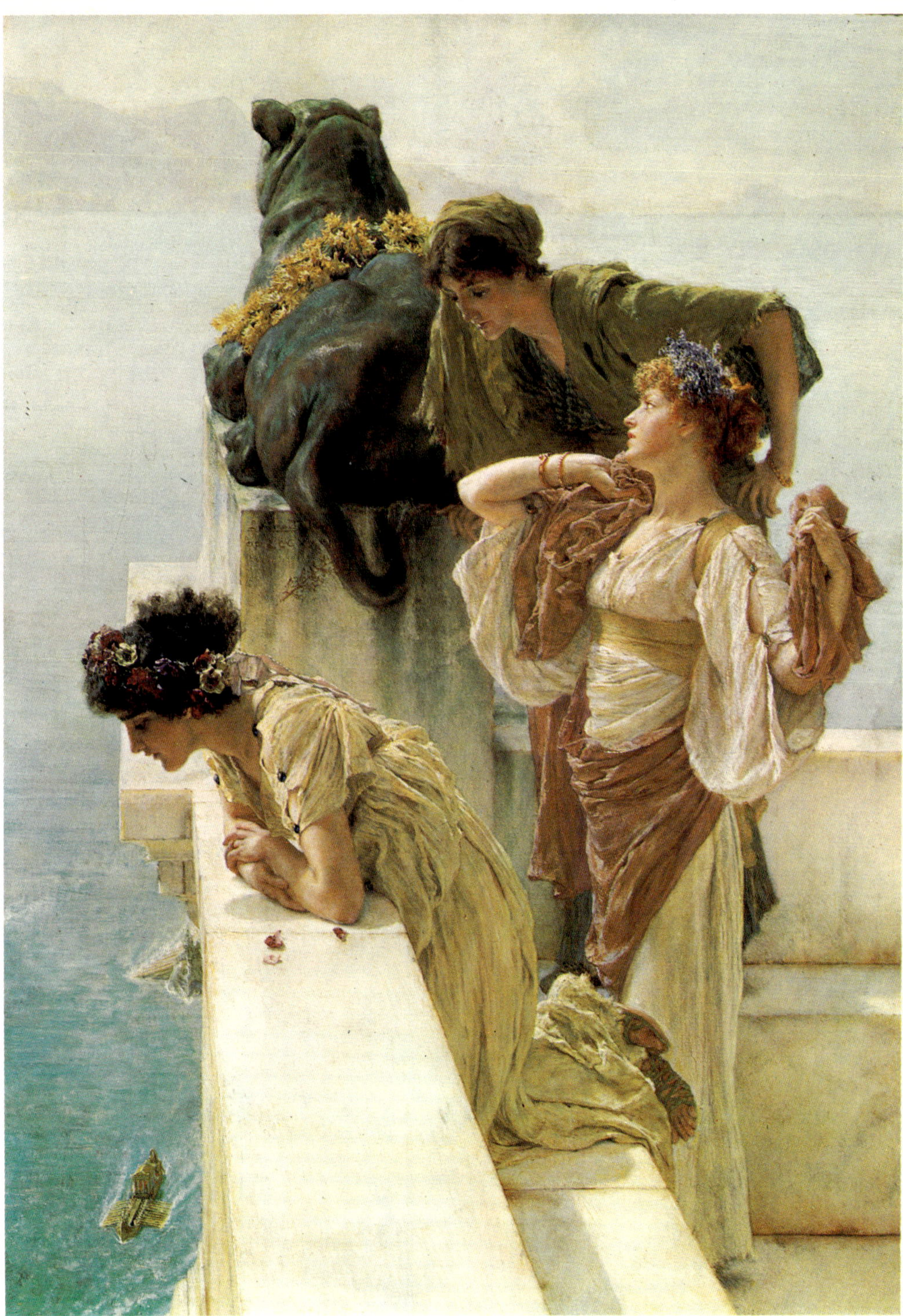

38

*The Baths of Caracalla
(Thermae Antoninianae)*
1899 Op. CCCLVI
60x37½ in

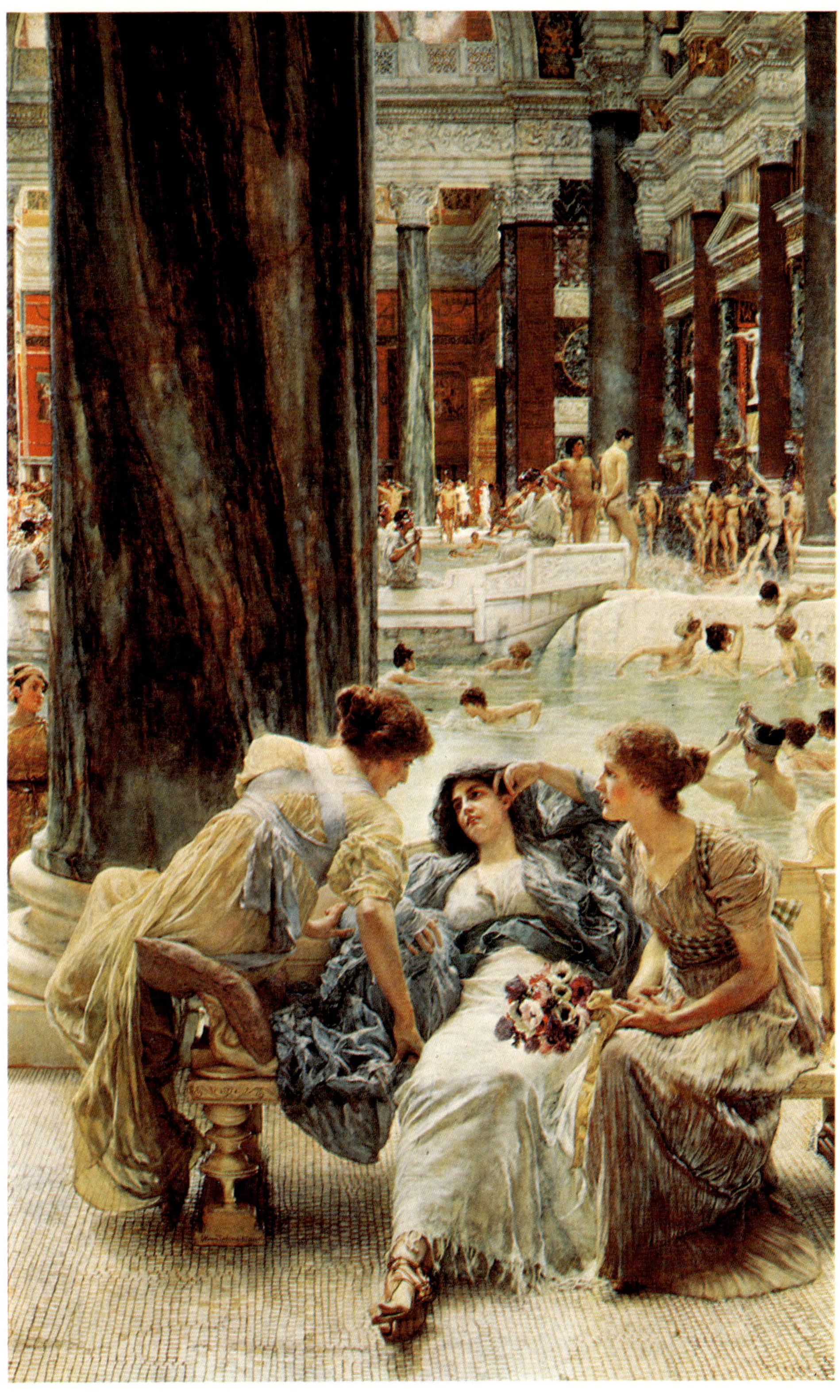

39

Vain Courtship
1900 Op. CCCLXII
30½x16¼ in

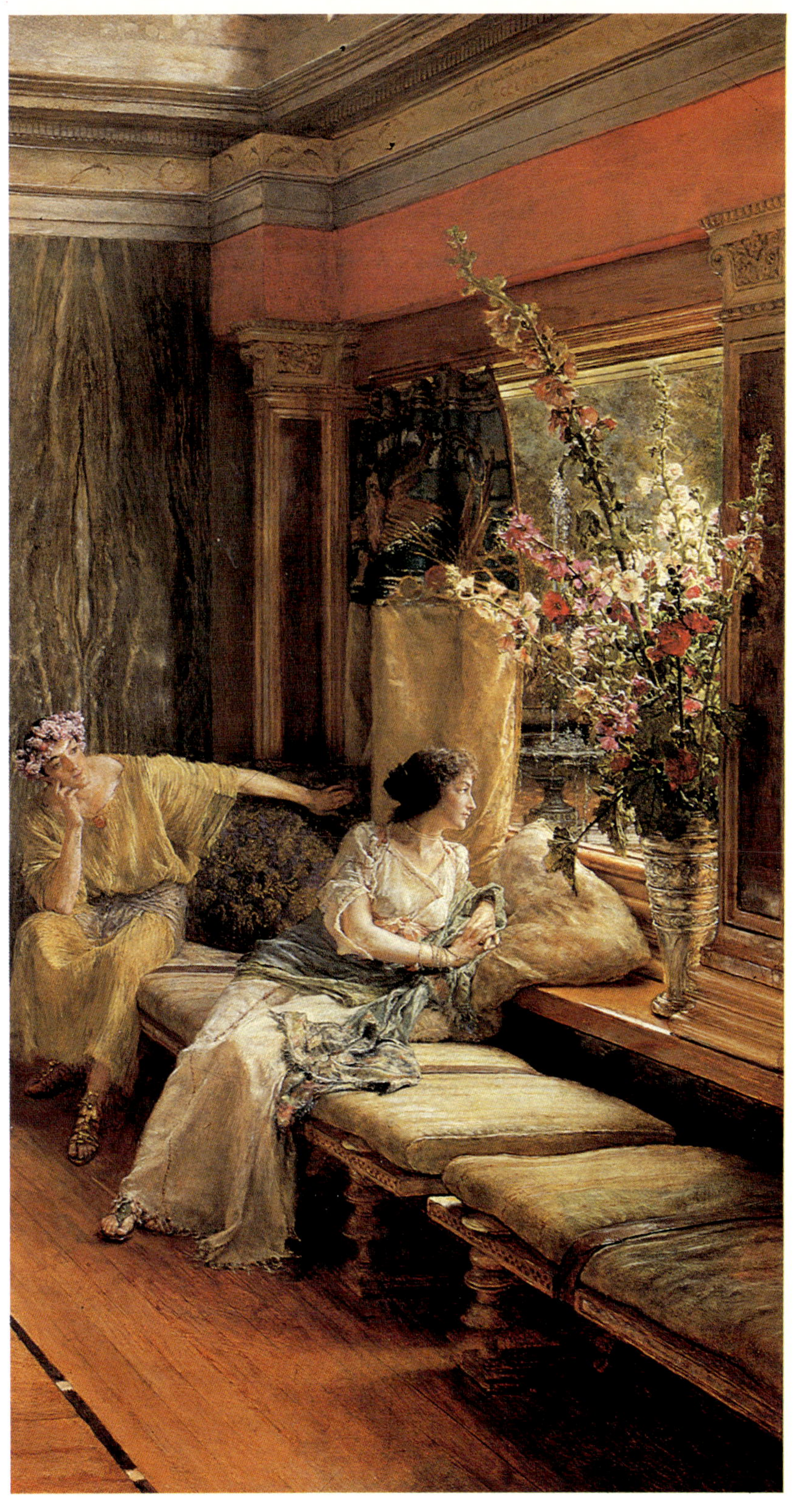

40

'The Year's at the Spring,
All's Right with the World.' (Browning)
1902 Op. CCCLXIX
13½x9½ in

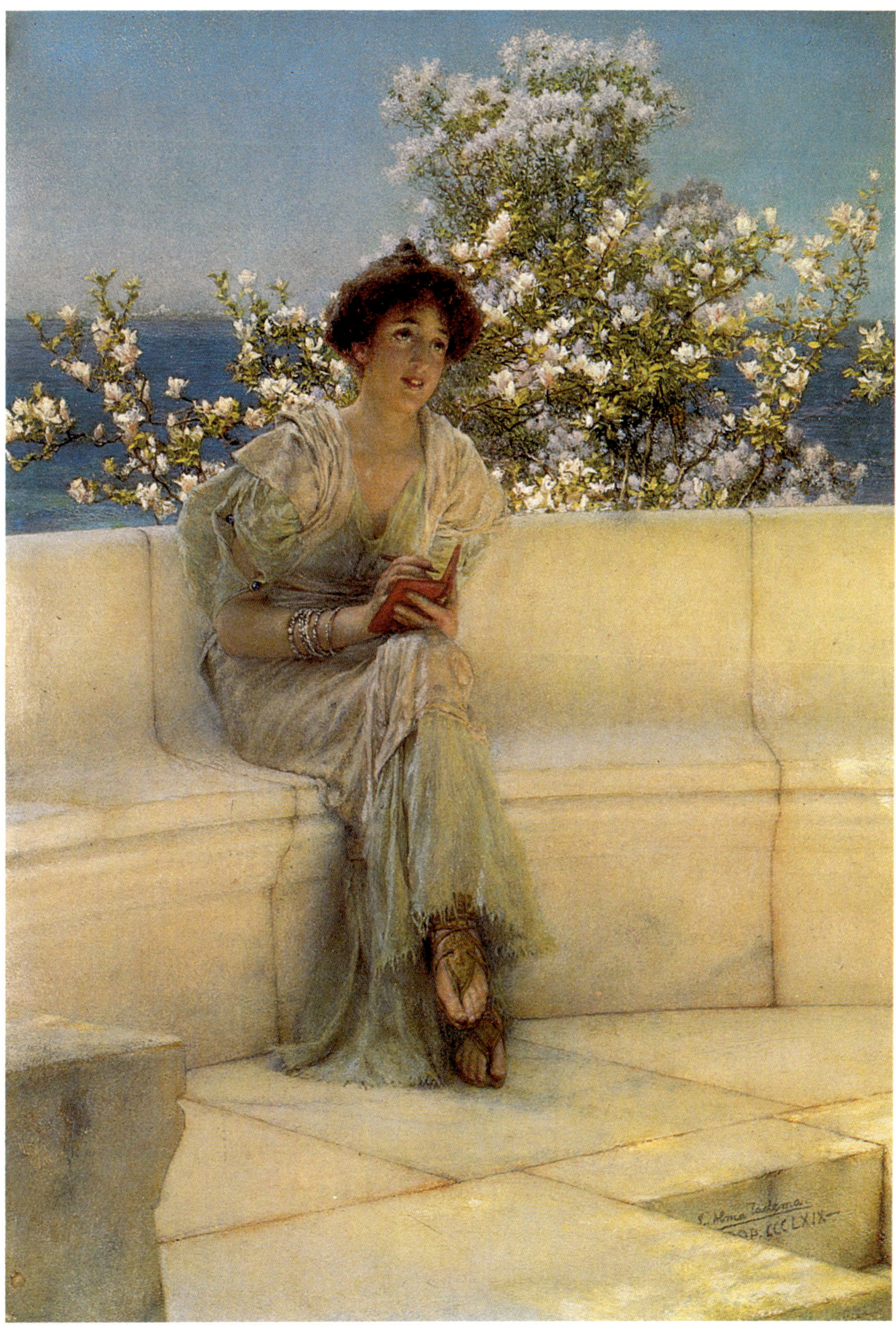

41

Caracalla
1902 Op. CCCLXX
9¼x15½ in

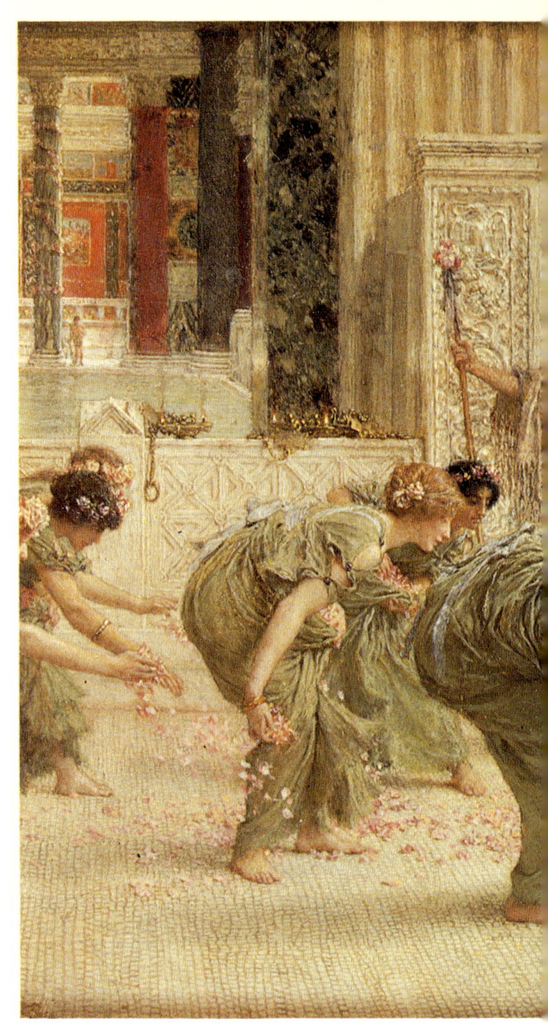

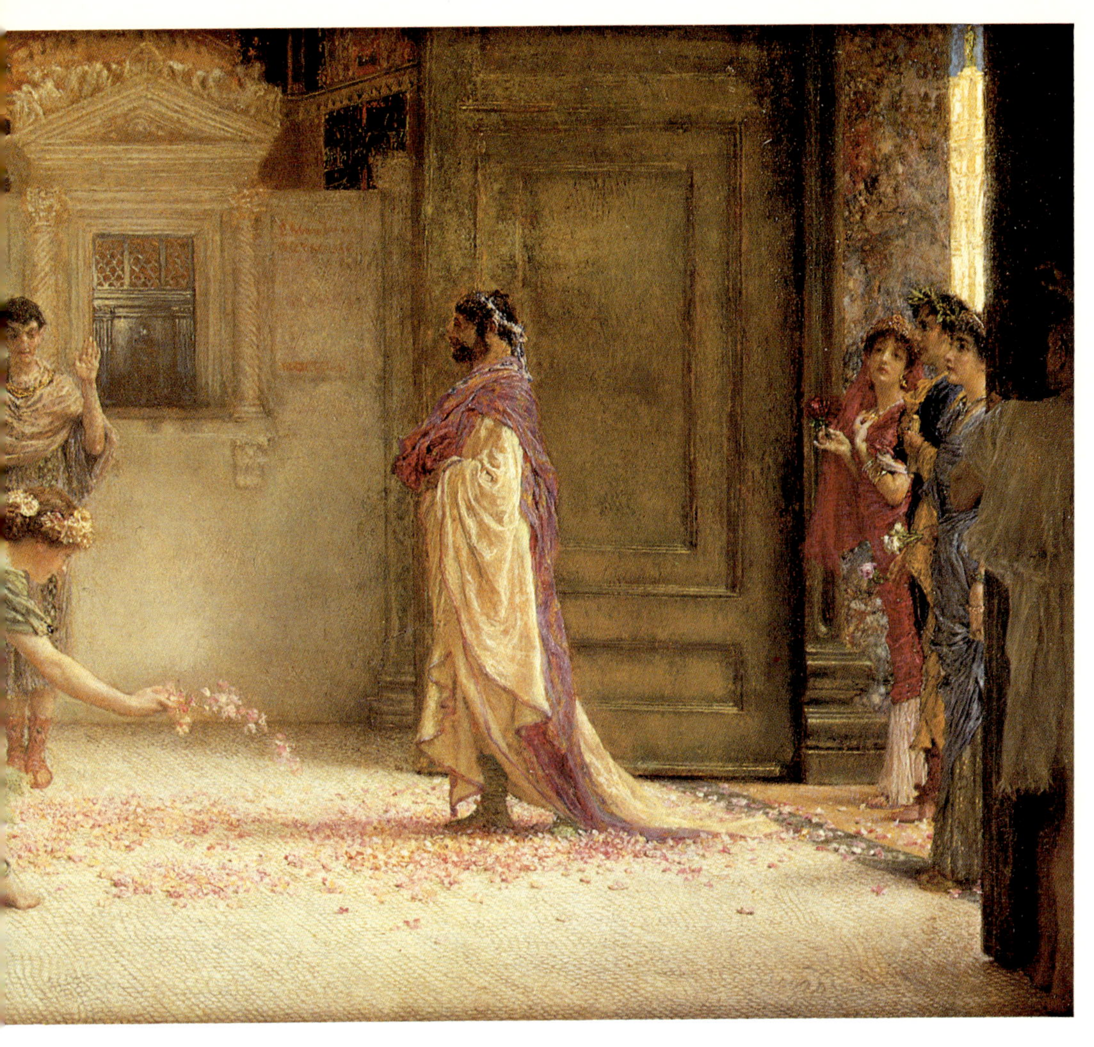

42

Silver Favourites (detail)
1903 Op. CCCLXXIII
27½x16¾ in

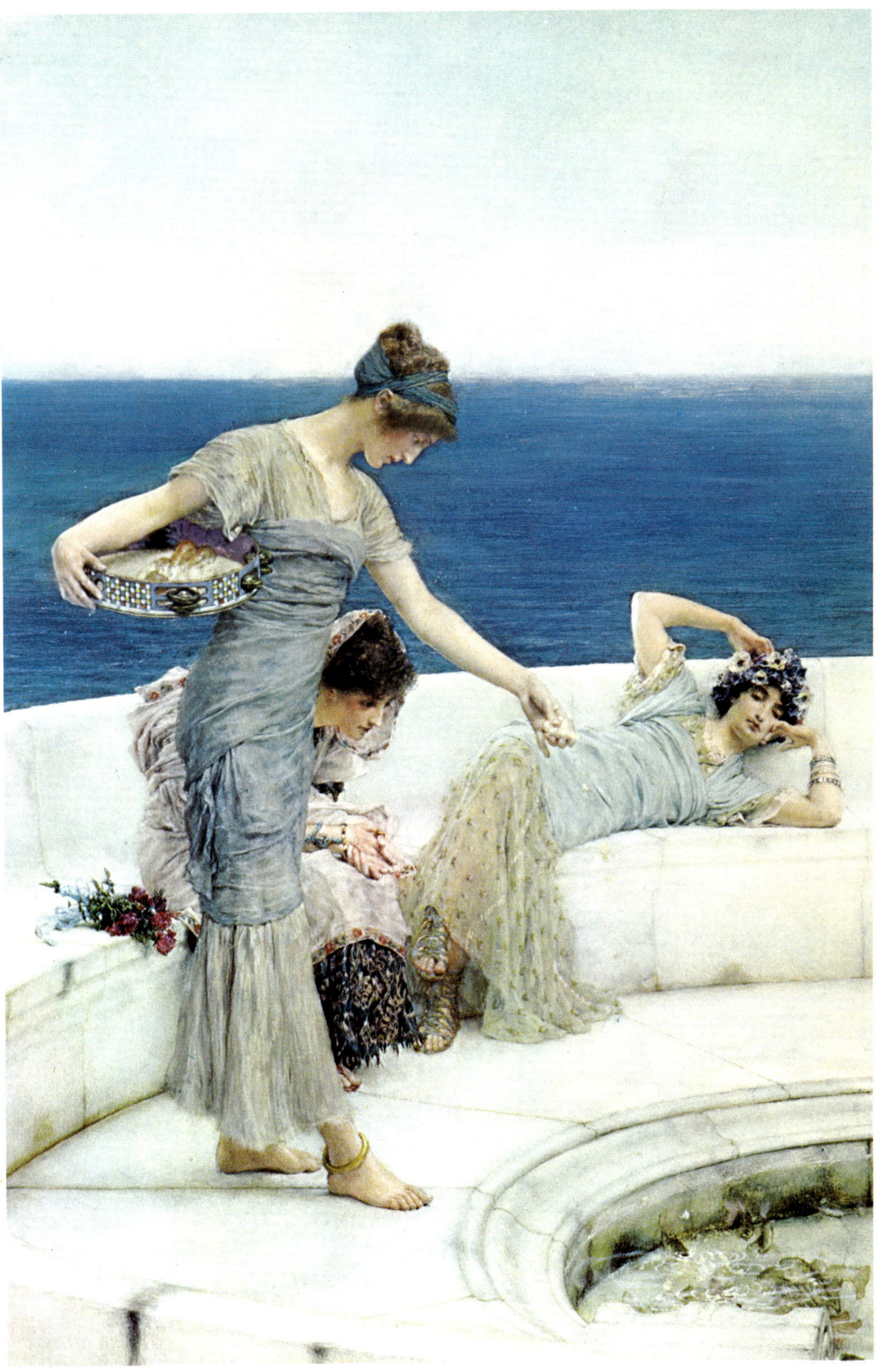

43

The Finding of Moses
1904 Op. CCCLXXVII
54x84 in

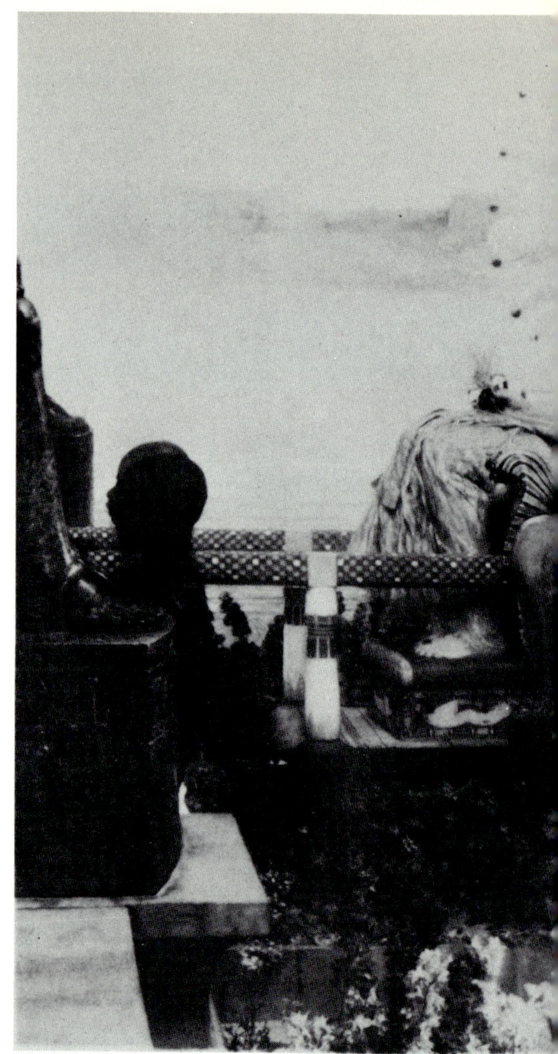

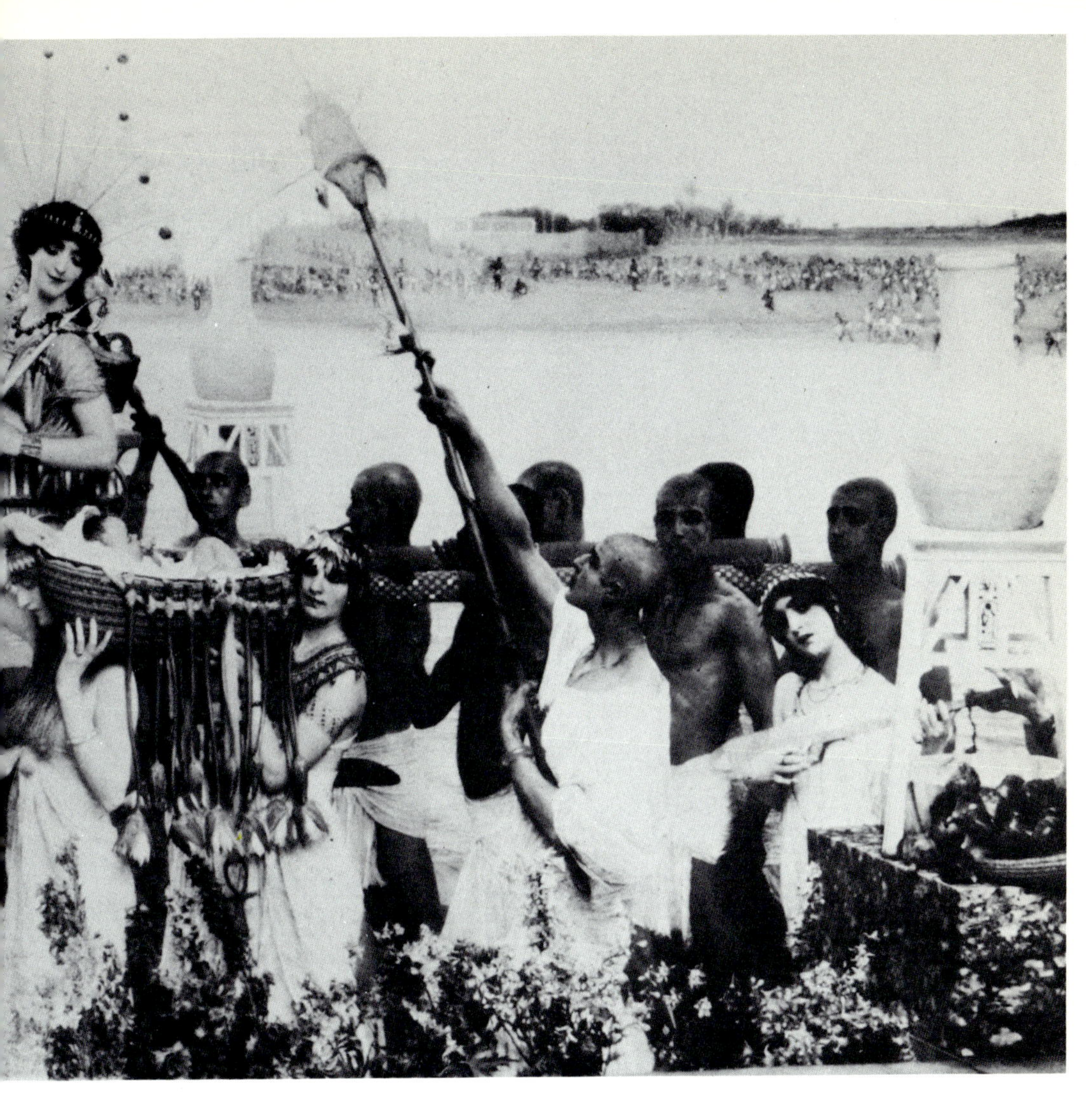

44

The Finding of Moses
(detail)

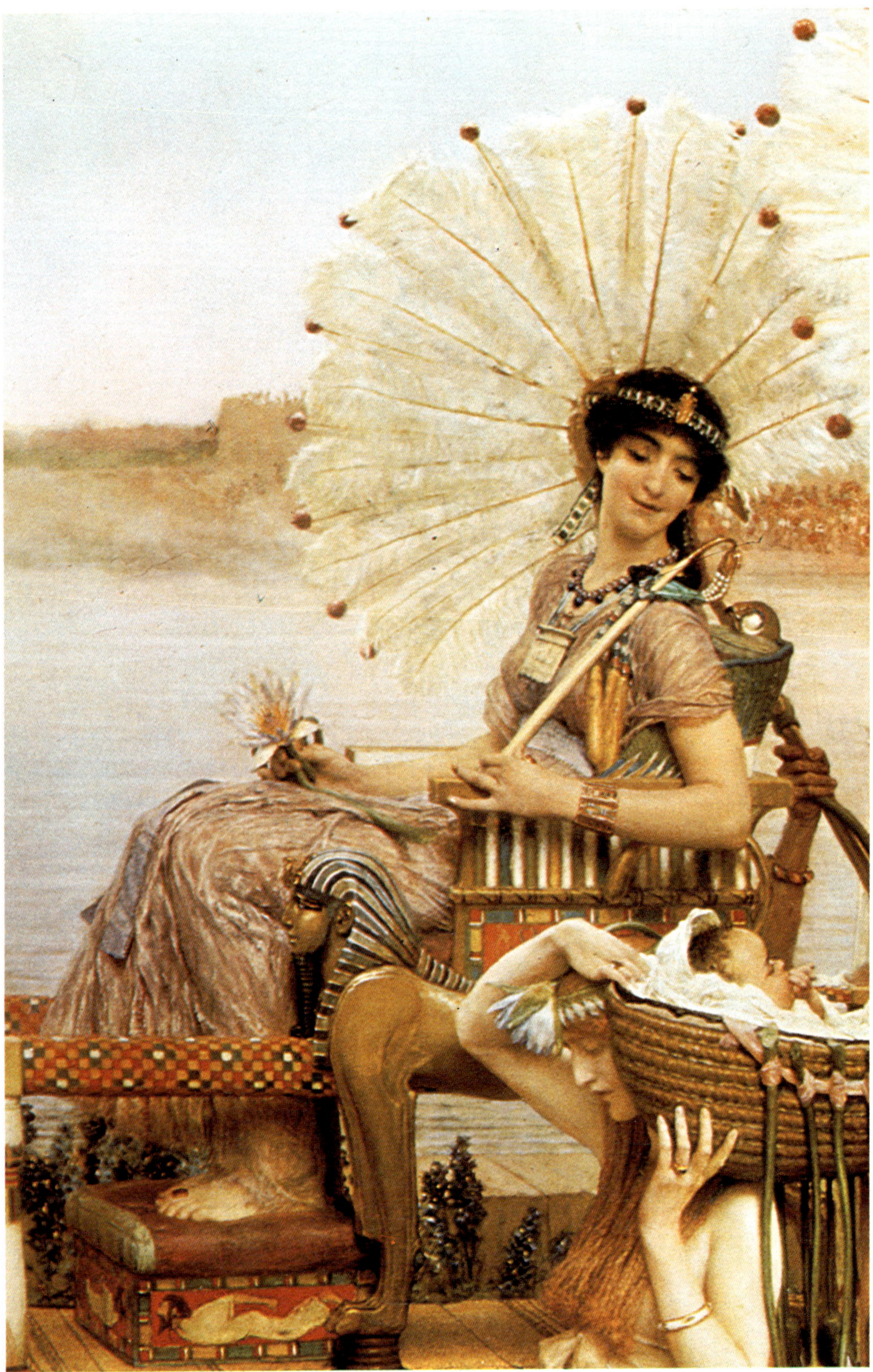

45

Orante
1907 Op. CCCLXXXIII
16¼x13 in

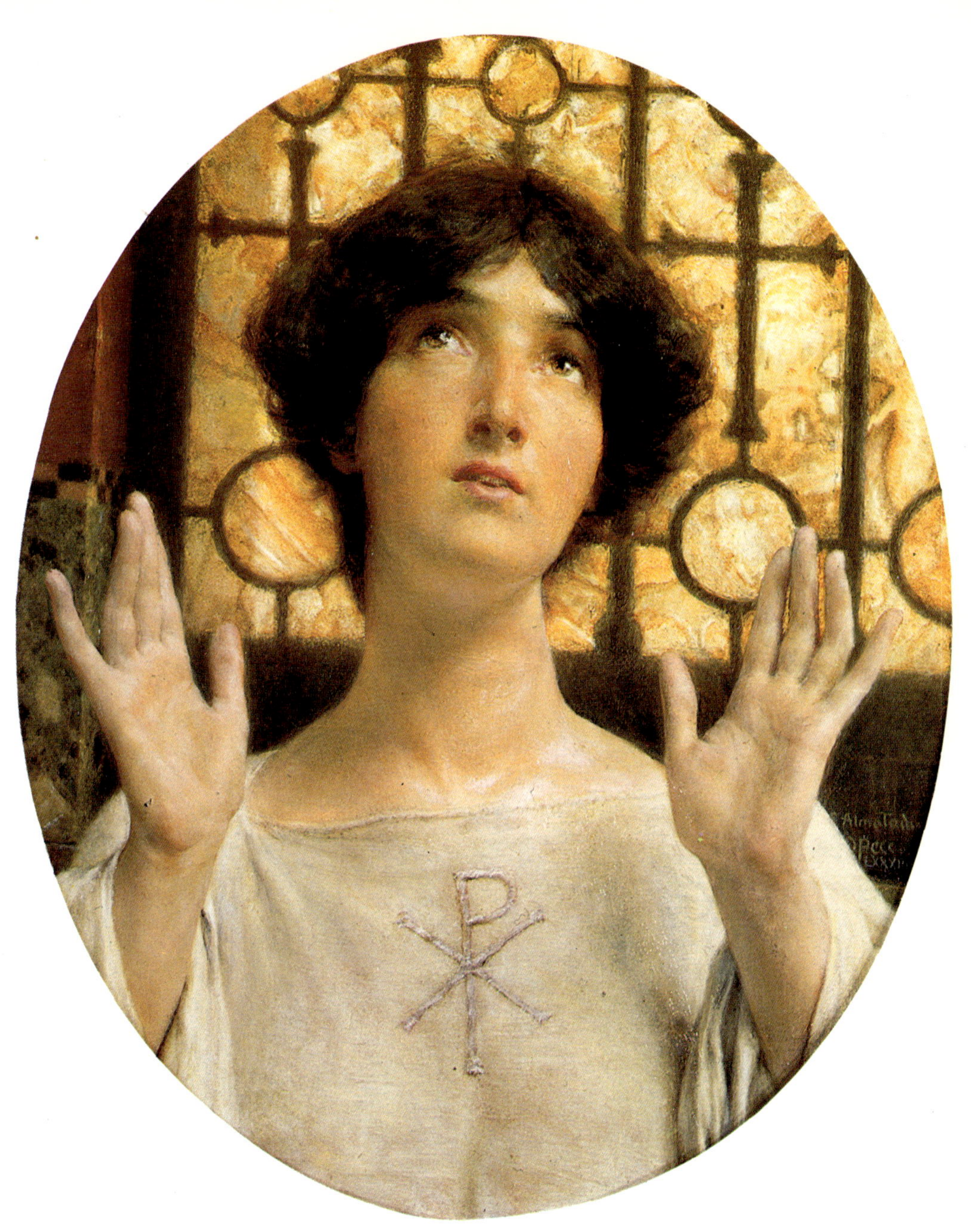

46 *Bacchante*
1907 Op. CCCLXXXIV
16¼x13¼ in

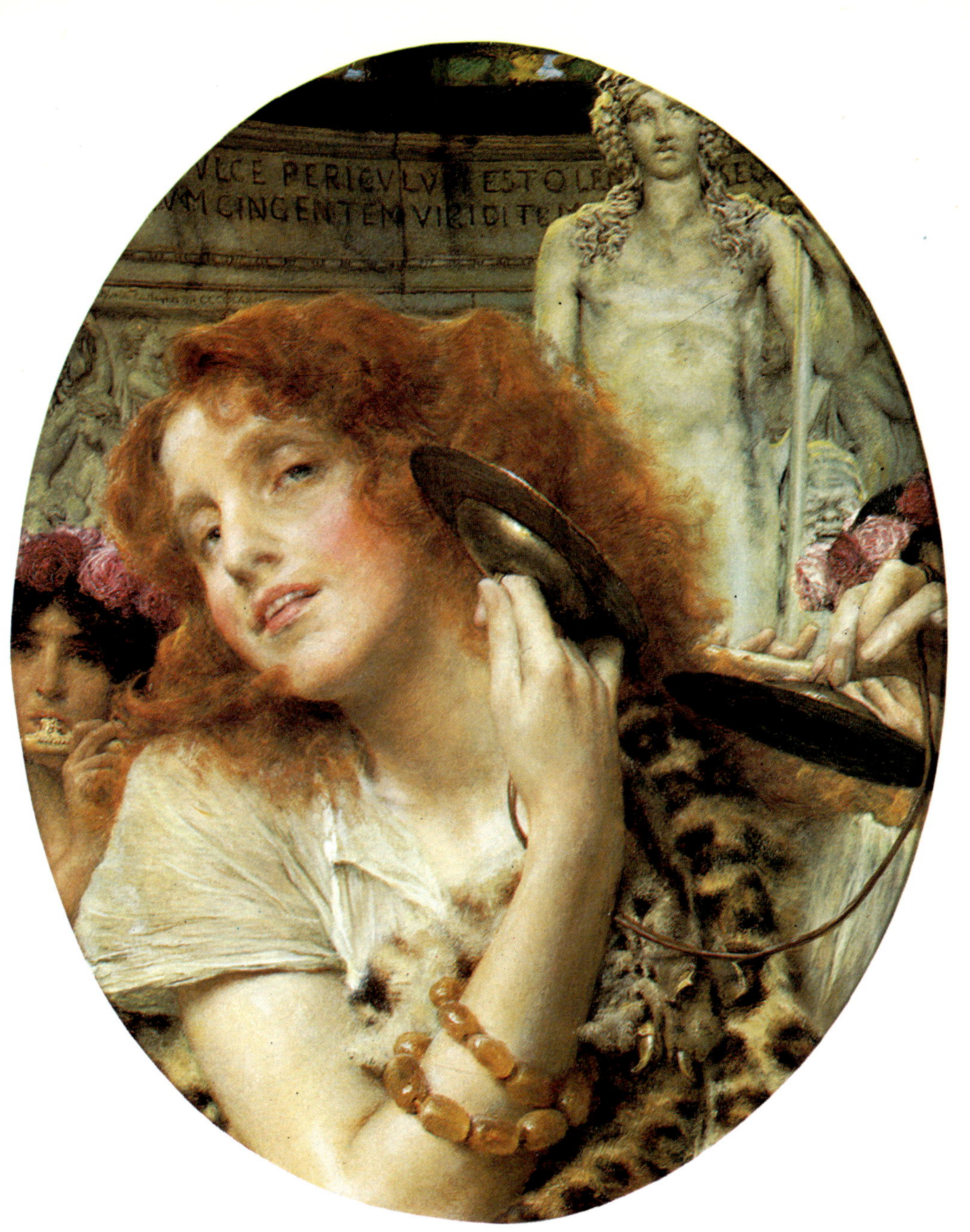
VLCE PERICVLVM EST O L
VM CINGENTEM VIRIDI TE

47

The Golden Hour
1907 Op. CCCLXXXVIII
14x14 in

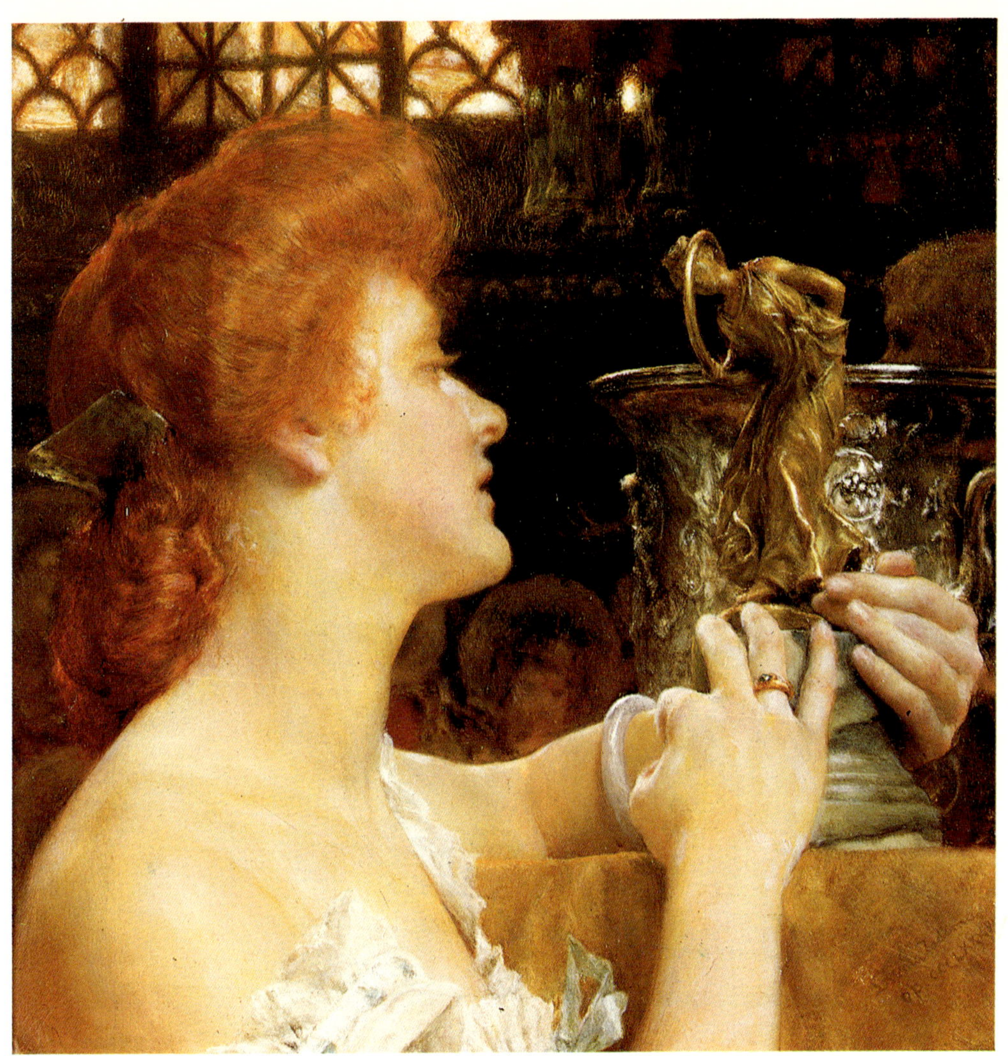

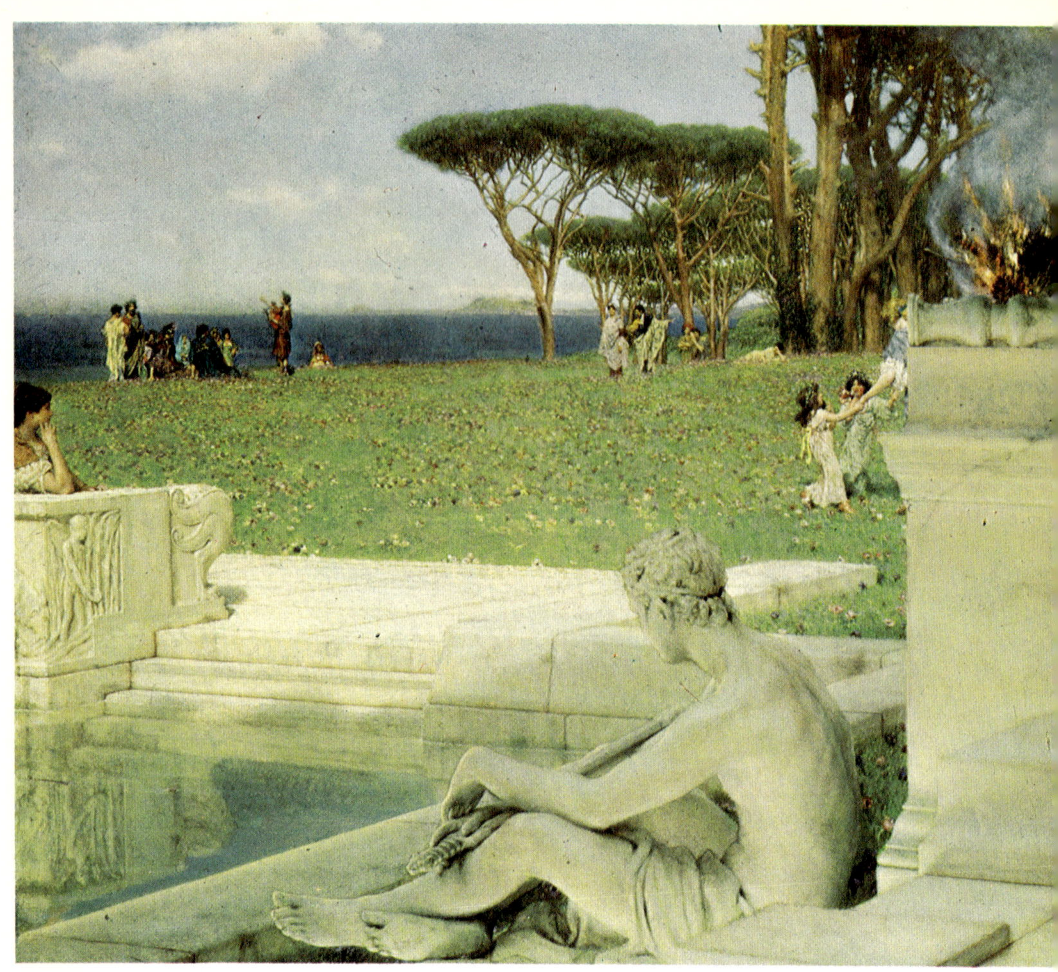

48

The Voice of Spring
1910 Op. CCCXCVII
19x45¼ in

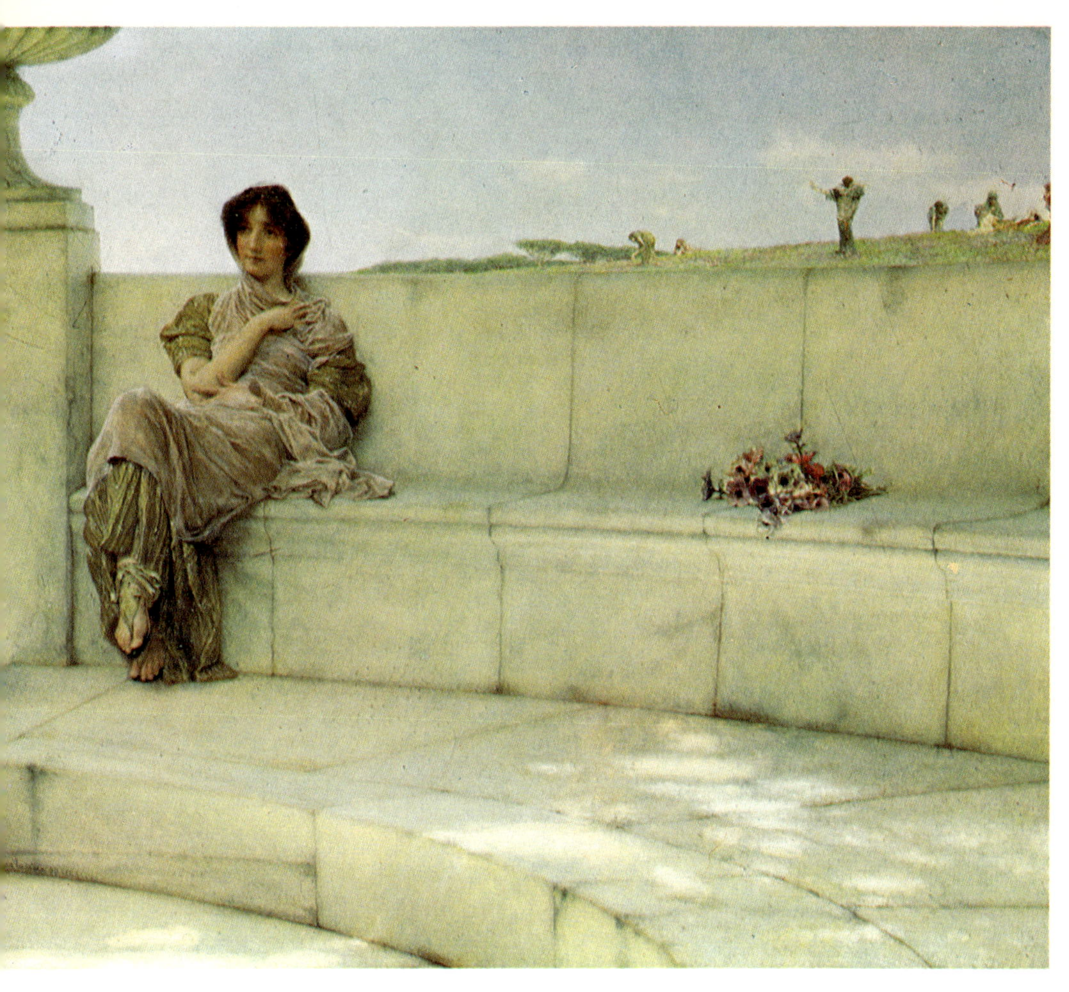